Can't Smack? Won't Smack?

New ways to bring harmony to families – And why the old ways don't work

Noël Janis-Norton

Barrington Stoke

First published in Great Britain by Barrington Stoke Ltd,
Sandeman House, 55 High Street, Edinburgh, EH1 1SR

www.barringtonstoke.co.uk

ISBN 1-84299-302-X

Edited by Julia Rowlandson
Cover design by Kate MacPhee
Typeset by GreenGate Publishing Services, Tonbridge, TN9 2RN
Printed in Great Britain by The Cromwell Press

Contents

Acknowledgements

I am profoundly grateful to my colleagues at The New Learning Centre, past and present, for their insight, sensitivity and commitment, and for sharing my vision of calmer, easier, happier family life:

Heleni Achilleos
Nancy Albanese
George Atiase
Suzanne Burdon
Miriam Chachamu
Alison Clark
Steve Diedrick
Gill Dyer
Gillian Edwards
Michael Foulkes
Helen Gabriel
Anne Geraghty
Suzi Gold
Sara Gordon
Tina Grammaticas
Mary Halliday

Melissa Hood
Isabel Irish
Abraham Jacob
Jill Janis
Geoff Kayum
Sue Kumleben
Mary Lee-Wolf
Clare Lewis
Peter Mellor
Chrissy Merton
Alison Rasalingam
Michael Rose
Annie Saunders
Luke Scott
Robin Shaw
Dorian Yeo

And to the many others who have also contributed to this work, too numerous to mention, my thanks.

My deepest appreciation goes to my children, Jessica, Jordan and Chloé, for the constancy of their support, encouragement and love.

Special thanks to the tens of thousands of parents who have tried these new methods and reported back, "It works!". Their courage and honesty continue to touch me and inspire me.

I owe a huge debt to Dr Haim Ginott, from whose books I first learned about Descriptive Praise, and to Adele Faber and Elaine Mazlish, whose accessible and empowering books I have been recommending to parents for the past two decades.

This book is dedicated to all parents who are searching for a calmer, easier, happier life for their children and for themselves.

SECTION I The Old Ways

Chapter 1
You are not alone

Wanted:

Woman or man to work 24 hour shifts. Seven days a week, no holidays, low status, much criticism, little appreciation. Must be flexible, and possess managerial, intellectual, manual and personnel skills, endless energy and good ideas.

Life contract, no grievance procedure.

No qualification required, no training given, no pay.

This is a typical job description for a modern-day parent. Raising a family has always been challenging, but many professionals and parents agree that it is becoming more difficult with each passing decade. Without extended family living nearby, the pressure is on modern parents to fulfil an impossible number of roles. With both parents working longer and longer hours, routines that were once leisurely and more satisfying, such as cooking, eating and household chores, are increasingly experienced as hurried and stressful.

With the perceived threat of "stranger danger" ever escalating, the freedom to play and wander outdoors has been drastically curtailed. Lively, curious children are constantly underfoot, seeking adventure and excitement in a small house or flat. Normal noisy, rambunctious play can be the last straw for a parent who is trying to unwind from a rushed, stress-filled day. Modern telecommunications have made it almost impossible to ever completely switch off. Television, video games and computers have crept into every corner of our homes, introducing seductive values and habits that parents struggle unsuccessfully to repel. The increased availability of inexpensive, unhealthy foods (high-sugar, high-fat and high-salt) has left parents and children at the same time more wired and also more lethargic.

In a job market that is perceived as increasingly cut-throat, many parents believe that education is the key to a good future for their children, but feel largely powerless to help their children be (and feel) successful academically.

Given the job description of the modern parent, it is no wonder that many parents feel so stressed, and are driven to nagging, threatening, criticising, screaming ... and smacking. Parents desperately want to change their negative reactions but do not know how.

At the New Learning Centre we teach confused, frustrated parents new, more positive ways of disciplining their children and new ways of communicating with them. When they first come to us, many of these mothers and fathers feel they must be bad parents because their children are non-co-operative or defiant or destructive or deliberately hurtful.

Here are the words of one mother who tearfully admitted to us that she regularly shouted at her child and also smacked him – more than she felt was right. Her words echo those of many: "*I feel quite desperate. I've reached a point where I love, but no longer like my child very much. I blame myself for having such a short fuse with him. I blame my husband for being too soft. I blame the school for being too hard on him. I even blame my child for making me feel like a failure.*"

Some of the parents who come to us for help are almost afraid of their angry, explosive children. They try, unsuccessfully, to avoid confrontations by doing anything for an easy life. They do not insist on please and thank you, let them stay up until they fall asleep in front of the television, feed them only their favourite junk foods, and are lax about homework.

Other parents are dealing with much milder behaviour problems. Day after day they pretend not to notice minor misbehaviour, hoping it will blow over. But the minor misbehaviour too often escalates into major misbehaviour as the children make a career out of pushing the limits – testing, testing, testing. Sooner or later, of course, these parents lose their cool and shout, "Enough is enough". At this point the parents are so frustrated, having put up with far too much for far too long, that they tend to over-react in anger, making up new draconian rules on the spot or threatening consequences that they hope they won't have to enforce. This is often followed by guilt and another bout of pretending not to notice misbehaviour.

This vicious circle of inconsistency and extreme reactions unintentionally reinforces their children's misbehaviour. Clearly this form of discipline is not working for these families.

Recent research reveals that three out of four parents admit to having smacked their children. Most of these parents feel guilty. They keep smacking for several reasons:

- They may not know a better way.
- They may know in theory what to do differently, but they don't know how to stay calm enough in the face of persistent misbehaviour to do it consistently.

When upset parents are trying not to smack they may choose what seems to be a lesser evil: they criticise, threaten, blame and shout. I call this verbal smacking.

There is increasing pressure on the British Government to radically alter the law on smacking. Until recently the law has upheld a parent's right to use "reasonable chastisement". In November 2004 the law was slightly amended. It is still a parent's right to smack, as long as it does not leave a mark. Some people believe that the government's reluctance to ban smacking outright comes from their realisation that upset, stressed parents will continue to smack, even if it is against the law, unless they have a realistic alternative. Also, it is in no one's interest to criminalise parents. Clearly what is needed is an alternative to smacking that is both effective and respectful.

We often talk about discipline as something that a parent does *after* a child has misbehaved. But in fact effective discipline is much more than that. In its fullest sense, discipline refers to teaching our children the habits, skills and values that we believe are right and helping them to internalise these values. We need to be teaching and training:

- When things are going smoothly, before any misbehaviour has occurred
- When we notice that things are starting to go wrong.

The most powerful discipline tool that I have discovered is Descriptive Praise. It is effective at all three stages: prevention, early intervention and crisis management. Section II explains this new method in detail and answers questions frequently asked by parents. When parents start using this pro-active approach they very soon find that they are no longer nearly so stressed, no longer nearly so tempted to criticise, repeat, remind, threaten, bribe, shout … or smack.

Chapter 2
Arguments for smacking

It is important to explore thoroughly, honestly and compassionately all the possible reasons that parents voice when they defend or justify smacking. Only then can those of us who are anti-smacking have any hope of helping parents become willing to open their minds to, and then put into practice, alternative methods of discipline.

Some of the arguments below focus on the perceived benefits of smacking. Other arguments implicitly accept that smacking is not the most effective response but attempt to justify or excuse it, either in terms of fallible human nature or of historical precedent.

Perceived benefits

1 A child can easily ignore or tune out a parent who is explaining, reasoning or repeating, but a smack will immediately get the child's attention. This is particularly true of a child who is over-tired, over-excited or upset.

2 When danger is imminent, there is no time for explanation.

3 The young child does not understand reasoning, but he does understand about avoiding pain.

4 When children understand but reject the parent's reasoning, corporal punishment gives them something they find hard to reject, namely pain.

5 Corporal punishment shows the child instantly that the parent is serious and is upset by the misbehaviour.

6 A smack is quicker and more immediate than any other form of punishment; therefore it is more likely to happen before the parent gets side-tracked.

7 A quick smack that instantly stops the misbehaviour is far preferable to a long, drawn-out process of reasoning, pleading, repeating and negotiating that gives the child the upper hand and allows him to continue to misbehave for longer.

8 Children's behaviour has deteriorated in recent decades as parents smack less. Similarly, the behaviour of pupils at school has

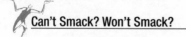

deteriorated because teachers are no longer allowed to administer, or threaten pupils with, physical punishment.

The next chapter and the rest of this book will show that these perceived benefits are illusory.

Justifications

1 At one time or another, most parents have smacked their children, even parents who are against smacking in principle.

2 In most families smacking is a rare occurrence. On balance, a child is left with far more happy, pleasant memories. This is another way to say, "It didn't do me any harm".

3 Most of the smacking happens when children are toddlers and preschoolers. As they grow up, they do not even remember the smacks.

4 Historical records tell us that parents have used corporal punishment since the dawn of time. For example, the Christian Bible (King James Version) says, "Spare the rod and spoil the child". Certain religious organisations still maintain that it is the only way to inculcate moral values in the mind of a child.

5 Each culture on the globe has evolved its own way of disciplining children. Who is to say that one way is better than another? (This stance is known as "cultural relativism".)

6 Children are naturally exasperating. No parent can have perfect self-control all the time. Spontaneously smacking a disobedient child is a natural human reaction.

7 Some children drive parents to distraction, for example children who are very active, noisy and impulsive.

8 Some parents are just too quick-tempered to be able to control themselves, no matter how hard they try.

9 Within the last century the pendulum of public opinion has swung from strict parenting all the way to permissive parenting and has started heading back towards strict again. Who can say which style is right and which is wrong?

10 Unquestionably, beating children is absolutely wrong. But an occasional smack by a loving parent is not the same as a beating. For many parents there are guidelines that govern smacking and keep it within acceptable limits. Although there is not universal agreement about these limits, here are the most widely quoted guidelines:

a A smack should be a last resort, to be used only after gentler methods have proven ineffective. Therefore it will happen infrequently.

b It should not leave a physical mark.

c It should not be done in anger or frustration, but to make an important point (e.g. "Don't cross the road without an adult," "Don't play with knives," "Don't hit the baby".)

d A smack should only be delivered by an adult whom the child loves and trusts.

e Smacking should be reserved for repeated defiance or for dangerous actions.

f Smacks should be administered in private. Smacking a child publicly is also humiliating.

g Parents should never use an object. Some parents would say that a soft object (such as a slipper) is acceptable, while a hard object (such as a belt or stick) is not.

h The smack should be delivered with an open hand, never with a fist.

i Parents should never hit a child on the face because it can be very painful and extra humiliating.

j The smack should be not much more than a tap; it should not really hurt.

In my opinion, the most useful thing that can be said in justification of smacking is that it is perfectly understandable why a stressed parent might resort to it. So those of us who are anti-smacking need to help vulnerable parents to feel less stressed and to put into practice effective methods for gaining co-operation.

Chapter 3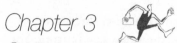
Arguments against smacking

In this chapter I have gathered together the reasons that many people put forward for why they are against smacking. I have avoided taking a moral stance. Instead, I have concentrated on showing that smacking is ineffective or unnecessary.

1 Smacking generates a distrust of and possibly even fear of the parent. This is true even if the child is hit only infrequently.

2 Children imitate their parents. Smacking sets the example that it is acceptable to use force, violence or intimidation as a solution to problems and as a way to get what you want. The strongest wins. The child who identifies with the parent's power may become a bully.

3 Hitting an adult is a crime. We all agree that it is not right. Children are more vulnerable than adults and therefore in even greater need of protection.

4 If the smacking is infrequent, as is usually the case, then by definition it is an inconsistent method of discipline. When repeatedly faced with inconsistent consequences, children respond by continually testing. They need to be able to predict how their parents will react as they can only feel secure and make sense of the world when they know the limits.

5 Some children keep getting smacked for the same misbehaviour. Clearly, the punishment is not effective at reducing the incidence of the misbehaviour. These children are either unable or unwilling to change their behaviour when reprimanded.

6 Children often remember the physical punishment but do not remember what misbehaviour led to it. The physical shock to the system of a smack seems to wipe that memory from their brain (in much the same way that accident victims often have amnesia about the events immediately preceding the accident).

7 Punishment reinforces children's immature, black and white, tit-for-tat thinking. Once the child has "taken" his punishment, he may now feel free to misbehave again.

8 We assume, or hope, that strong punishment teaches a child what he should not do. As we have seen, that is often not the case. But even if he has learned what *not* to do, he has not learned anything about:
- Why his behaviour was so upsetting to the parent
- How to plan ahead to avoid similar situations
- How to think about alternative courses of action
- How to harness, re-direct or control his impulses
- How to make amends in any real sense.

If these issues are addressed, punishment is unnecessary or can be much milder and still be effective.

9 Boys get smacked and shouted at more than girls. This is because boys, more than girls, exhibit characteristics that tend to annoy a parent, e.g.
- loud voice
- not answering a parent's questions
- reacting slowly when told to stop
- moving a lot, touching objects, fiddling and fidgeting.

A boy should not be punished for behaviour that is clearly part of being a boy.

10 The child who typically gets punished a lot is by nature particularly boisterous, loud, immature, slow to comply, and quick to get upset. This child does not yet know how to control his actions and reactions, especially when he is hungry, tired, upset or absorbed in something. Punishment cannot teach him this important self-control.

11 With a relatively easy-going child, who does not get upset easily and who is more able to control his impulses, smacking might seem to work. But smacking is not "necessary" with such children because they respond very well to other approaches.

12 Some advocates of smacking say that in order to keep the smack light parents should never smack in anger. But generally it is only when very angry that parents *do* smack. It is tempting to smack with more force because if the smack is not hard enough to hurt or insult, it will not be a deterrent.

13 Most parents would not tolerate an adult from outside the family smacking, shouting at or even criticising their child. Is the child the parent's property to do with as he wishes? Society once believed that it was acceptable for husbands to hit their wives because they were their "property". We no longer find this acceptable.

14 Even parents who believe that smacking is acceptable only find themselves resorting to it when they are particularly stressed. Most smacks are not administered for major misbehaviour but for day-to-day minor misbehaviour. When stresses are reduced and parents feel calmer, they deal with the misbehaviour more calmly. They automatically choose non-smacking forms of discipline and universally report that these are far more effective.

15 Even parents for whom smacking is acceptable rarely choose to smack as their initial response to misbehaviour. They try other approaches first, in the hope that smacking will not be "necessary". Often, they issue threats of a smack, of withdrawal of a privilege or of removing the object in dispute. Desperate parents often repeat the threats, hoping that will be enough to stop the behaviour so that they will not have to follow through. The threats may stop the misbehaviour for a few minutes at best, but when the beleaguered parent has finally "had enough" and reacts with a smack, the child is justifiably outraged. All those repetitions of the threat have led the child, understandably, not to take what the parents say seriously. As far as the child is concerned, the interaction has developed into a game, in which it is the parent's role to repeat, remind, plead and threaten while it is the child's role to test and defy. The child has no understanding of why, when he is doing the same thing he was doing before, suddenly the parent decides to smack. The child does not understand the concept of "enough is enough" or "the last straw". The inconsistency puzzles and angers him, even though he often cannot express his upset coherently.

16 Typically a stressed parent who has just smacked, very quickly regrets the loss of self-control. Guilt sets in and with it a desire to apologise or make it up to the child, especially if the child is crying or sulking. An apology is of course preferable to insisting that the child drove you to it, but repeated apologies lose their effectiveness. The child comes to think, if not to say, "If you're so sorry, why do you keep doing it?". A child will lose respect for a parent who seems unable to control himself. After a parental outburst, guilt, coupled with the child's obvious upset, often drives the parent to be temporarily over-indulgent, giving in about issues he or she would normally stand firm on, or offering treats in an attempt to restore a harmonious atmosphere. The parent may also deliberately choose not to react to misbehaviour out of worry that he or she will again lose control. The swing between harsh, angry reactions at one end of the pendulum and over-indulgence at the other end results in an erratic, inconsistent style of parenting that is very confusing and frustrating for all concerned. A parent's guilt is very unsettling emotionally for a child because it gives him a power that he is far too young to know how to handle, namely power over an adult's feelings. Children need their parents to be solid, stable, and in charge. When the tables are turned and the child is emotionally in charge, he becomes increasingly anxious and resentful, and his behaviour deteriorates further. When a parent loses control, the child may see the parent as weak, possibly even as childish, and may lose respect. A vicious circle, fuelled by anger, is created.

17 We all have observed that children who do not get enough positive attention soon become experts at getting negative attention. Smacking and shouting can become, in the child's eyes, substitutes for affection and approval. When this reversal of emotions prevails, punishment loses all its potential deterrent effect. The child no longer tries to avoid punishment. In fact, he may actively invite and welcome punishment, as a sign that the parents care enough to get upset and to pay attention to him.

18 Schools are no longer allowed to use corporal punishment because we know that it breeds resentment without improving behaviour. Back in the days when caning was the norm, the same pupils got caned again and again, year after year (just as nowadays the same pupils keep getting detentions).

19 Some children exhibit, often as part of their inborn temperament, an unusually strong urge to engage in activities that are physically challenging or aggression-laden, that involve a high degree of risk, and that are exciting or forbidden. Such a child is driven by this urge and cannot easily stop himself, no matter how much he is motivated to avoid pain or humiliation. He needs a different approach, one that can ease him gradually into better habits. Baiting or defying a potentially explosive parent or teacher to see, if and when, she can be pushed over the edge can become a favourite pastime, as addictive a "game" as any violent computer game. Even getting hit can eventually be experienced as part of the excitement. Children can become masters at befuddling and infuriating the adults by "bending" the rules (rather than breaking them), by following the letter of the law while violating the spirit of the law, by exploiting loopholes, lying, getting others in trouble, citing obscure and irrelevant precedents and arguing about inconsequential aspects of the matter. These children are often highly competitive, and paradoxically, they may feel that they have won, regardless of how the "game" turns out. Whether they manage to evade punishment or to provoke the adult into screaming or smacking, they experience that sense of satisfaction that comes from accomplishing what one set out to do.

20 In my professional experience, the vast majority of children who are smacked more than once or twice a year turn out later to be diagnosed with a subtle specific learning difficulty that impairs their
  – ability to concentrate
  – auditory memory
  – organisational skills
  – social skills
  – ability to wait patiently
  – speech and language
  – fine-motor skills.

The guilt-ridden parent of a child with these characteristics will be relieved to learn that the smacking did not cause the learning difficulty; nor did the shouting, telling off and nagging. A learning difficulty is part of the child's genetic make-up, often linked to a sensitive, intense, impulsive nature. Although hard-wired from before birth, the characteristics mentioned above ordinarily only become apparent once the baby is mobile. As soon as he can crawl, he is "into everything", spurred on by a seemingly unquenchable urge to touch, hold, put in his mouth or dismantle everything that catches his interest.

Even though this child may be bright, parents notice that he matures more slowly than his peers do. Long after others of his age are feeding and dressing themselves, playing independently, saying please and thank you, using the toilet and learning the alphabet, this child's responses are still very hit or miss. Sometimes he remembers; sometimes he doesn't. Sometimes it seems that he can't be bothered to do the right thing; sometimes it looks like pure defiance.

It is very easy to become exasperated with a child who seems to ignore you or even to enjoy winding you up. It is easy to lose control or to decide that you need to assert your authority "once and for all". This is how the parental habit of shouting, threatening, telling off, nagging and eventually smacking takes root. It is both unfair and completely ineffective to punish the child for his immature or impaired functioning.

21 Studies have shown that even in warm, loving families, a child receives approximately nine criticisms for each sentence of approval or appreciation. For further discussion of this, see Chapter 4, "What we mean by "verbal smacking?" As a result of this imbalance, with negative attention far outweighing positive attention, a vicious circle is created, which becomes even more pronounced when shouting and smacking are added to the nagging and criticising. The child's annoying behaviour leads to the parent reacting negatively, which leads to the child misbehaving even more, which leads to more parental "misbehaviour". No amount of punishing and telling off can break this cycle.

22 A child who is punished or told off frequently, may come to see himself as bad. It may seem only right to this child that he be punished. Over the years, his tolerance level for punishment increases. It may look to the frustrated, furious parent as if the child just does not care or get upset about punishment. But the fact is that he has accepted this way of life as his just deserts. He believes that he deserves to be punished or told off, and he may even become distinctly uncomfortable when praised or rewarded.

23 We often see a situation in which one parent becomes very angry and starts to shout, threaten or punish, while the other parent remains relatively calm in relation to the children but gets angry at the parent who is losing control. In some families these roles are generally static, while in other families the roles might be reversed on a different day. In either case the lack of unity between the parents leaves the child with a lot of room for manoeuvring. He can get what he wants or "get away with" misbehaviour by playing one parent off against the other. This child may learn how to get one parent "in trouble" with the other. Exercising this heady power leads to guilt, which adversely affects the child's self-esteem.

24 By and large it is the impulsive, easily upset parent who smacks too hard or too often. As a child, this parent was, himself, smacked too hard and too often by parents who could not cope with his difficult temperament. This has resulted in emotional "baggage", feelings of resentment and helplessness, which may not rise to the surface until he is faced with a child similar to himself, a child who often misbehaves or disobeys or is simply too noisy or demanding or easily upset. This parent has never learned how to control his or her own inappropriate impulses and is passing this dangerous legacy on to the next generation.

25 Children become afraid or anxious, as well as resentful, when they have been hurt, humiliated or threatened with hurt or humiliation. We now know, from recent brain research, that in an anxious state the brain releases chemicals, notably cortisol, that temporarily paralyse many of the higher-level functions of the frontal cortex, effectively blocking reasoning and mature learning. What learning is still able to take place has been termed "survival learning". The child who has been hurt or humiliated learns survival behaviour. At best, he learns to avoid getting caught by not repeating the misbehaviour when an adult is around.

26 When a child is frequently punished or criticised, he may start to sense that he is a terrible disappointment to his parents, that no matter how hard he tries, he always gets it wrong. Over time, he gives up trying. He comes to believe that it is his lot in life to be scolded, shouted at or smacked. No amount of further chastising will modify this child's view of himself and his world; in fact, it will only serve to further depress the child's low self-esteem.

Chapter 4
What we mean by "verbal smacking"

Most of us would not dream of smacking our children daily, weekly or even monthly. It is something that happens very, very rarely and which we almost instantly regret.

Yet we allow ourselves to "smack" our children with words, often daily, particularly when we are very stressed, which seems to be more and more of the time. The criticising, complaining, blaming, threatening and shouting that escape our lips qualify, in my opinion, as "verbal smacking".

For most families verbal smacking is much more of a problem than physical smacking because it is much more frequent and because parents do not instantly regret it. It seems to be almost taken for granted that our children will irritate and exasperate us so much that we are justified in snapping at them with annoyance, nagging them again and again, complaining, criticising and losing our tempers.

Research indicates that most smacking occurs when children are between the ages of 15 months and four years old. After that age, parents generally try to reason with the child, which is often ineffective. When reasoning fails, the frazzled parent slides inevitably into repeating, reminding, cajoling, bargaining, bribing, threatening, blaming, and then eventually shouting and possibly smacking. Neither child nor parent feels good, and the child does not learn to behave better.

Verbal smacks can hurt as much as physical smacks do. But parents may not realise this because children become adept at hiding their hurt under a layer of defiance, testing, whingeing and revenge. Verbal smacks decrease the likelihood of the child listening to us, respecting us and co-operating with us.

You may well recognise some of the pointless, counter-productive sentences which do not work to bring us the calm family life we want:

1 When children ignore us or argue back:
   "Why can't you just do what you're told?"
   "You have no respect."
   "The trouble with you is…"
   "You've got to learn to do as you're told."

"When are you going to learn to listen?"

"How dare you talk to me like that?"

"You're driving me crazy!"

"Act your age."

"O.K., as long as you promise me you'll clean your room just as soon as this programme is over."

"I'm getting cross now."

"You're giving me a headache."

"You do that one more time and then you'll go to your room."

"I mean it!"

"Can't you just behave?"

"Why can't you be like your sister?"

"That is completely unacceptable!"

"How many times have I told you…?"

"Don't make me smack you."

2 When children are actively exploring their environment in ways that make more work for us:

"Leave that alone."

"It's not a toy."

"That's not yours."

"You have no respect for private property."

"You'll hurt yourself."

"I was waiting for that to happen."

"That's breakable."

"Watch where you're going."

"Didn't I tell you to stop?"

"Be careful!"

"If I catch you doing that one more time…"

"Why did you do that?"

3 When they get distracted:

"Hurry up."

"You're making us late."

"I don't have all day."

"Why are you always the last one ready?"

"You would forget your head if it wasn't screwed on."

4 When they are reluctant or self-conscious:

"You'll live."

"Why do you have to make such a fuss about everything?"

"Now that wasn't so bad, was it?"

5 When siblings squabble:

"You're older; you should know better."

"I don't want to hear about it."

"You can kill each other for all I care."

"Can't you keep your hands to yourself?"

"How would you like it if someone did that to you?"

"Ignore him and he'll stop."

"Sit next to me, then he won't bother you."

"Just walk away."

"Act like you don't care."

"If you get upset, he'll do it even more."

Here is another form of verbal smacking, labels that hurt and do not work to draw out the best in our children:

"You are...

aggressive	inconsiderate
annoying	jealous
babyish	lazy
bad	manipulative
bossy	messy
a brat	moody
careless	naughty
clumsy	over-reacting
a cry baby	over-sensitive
a dawdler	rude
daydreaming	selfish
demanding	show-off
difficult	shy
dishonest	a slowcoach
disrespectful	spoiled
disruptive	stubborn
distractible	thoughtless
a drama queen	unco-operative
forgetful	unco-ordinated
fussy	ungrateful
greedy	wilful".

Many children hear just a few of these counter-productive sentences or labels occasionally, and not much damage is done. But some children hear words like these most days. These are often the children who are particularly sensitive, intense, impulsive and noisy. These children seem to bring out the worst in parents and teachers. Daily repetition of these criticisms and complaints not only erodes a child's self-esteem but also his willingness to listen and co-operate.

Think back to when you were a child. How did you feel when you were told off or punished? Did it motivate you to improve, or did it make you feel angry, threatened, deflated or hopeless? If you can't remember, think of some times in your adult life when you were criticised. The experience usually triggers defensiveness, shame or possibly a counter-attack, but rarely does it empower us to do our best.

It doesn't have to be like this.

Chapter 5

Why parents smack, shout, tell off and nag, even when these reactions do not improve behaviour

These parents spoke for many when they said:

- "I used to regularly scream at my children around bedtime. And, like clockwork, as soon as they were finally asleep, I would slump onto the sofa, almost in tears, so frustrated and so ashamed of myself. It happened so many evenings. I would vow to be more patient and calm. What I didn't realise back then was that I didn't have a clue how to get them to do what I asked. So I was making a vow that I just couldn't keep."

- "It's how I was brought up. It just seemed natural to me to remind and remind and remind and then after a while threaten and then finally scream at them to stop. They did stop then, but they looked scared, which made me feel very guilty."

- "I used to feel so powerless when my children wound me up. I felt that by nagging them, I was at least trying to do something about the problem. But I could see that telling them off and shouting often just made matters worse. I kept hoping it would work this time."

- "I had no idea that there were things I could do to help my children want to behave well. So every day I would just wait for the usual misbehaviour. When they played up I tried to be patient. But then I would explode and shout. I wasn't proud of myself. I would tell myself: 'They're just children, not monsters'. But I always ended up losing my patience. They did seem like monsters!"

Even parents who believe that smacking is acceptable would rather not do it. They usually resort to smacking only out of extreme frustration, after their usual disciplinary techniques have repeatedly proved unsuccessful.

And parents who believe that smacking is wrong also find themselves at times feeling very frustrated, angry and helpless. Eventually, frayed tempers snap and then these parents may smack.

The negative labels and phrases from Chapter 4 may seem to be accurate descriptions of a child's weaknesses or bad habits. We grow up believing that it is useful to point out to people the areas in which they need to improve. We assume that if the child could only realise how he appears to others, especially when he gets a taste of how angry that makes people, surely that would motivate him to try harder. Unfortunately, criticism rarely motivates. Criticism is far more likely to backfire and leave the child feeling resentful, anxious or defeated. Children "live down" to these labels.

To an angry, frustrated parent who is feeling desperate, saying something cutting serves, albeit temporarily, to release some of the mounting tension, even though we all know from bitter experience that it is not effective. Once we cool down we feel guilty and regret having lost control, but we do not know how to stop ourselves. At the time, words of hurtful criticism seem infinitely preferable to a smack or a yank. We may be able to refrain, most of the time, from saying these hurtful things directly *to* our children, but we may use the labels when talking *about* the child, forgetting that children hear and understand far more than we generally give them credit for.

Chapter 6

Which behaviours provoke parents to smack, either physically or verbally

The main complaints about misbehaviour fall into two categories.

1 Stop behaviours – these are actions we want our children to stop doing, e.g.:
   - Whingeing or crying when they don't get what they want
   - Asking to be bought something each time we go to the shops
   - Climbing on the furniture
   - Throwing things in anger.

2 Start behaviours – the child is not misbehaving, but we want him to start doing something else, e.g.:
   - Putting toys away
   - Doing homework carefully
   - Going to bed
   - Trying a new food
   - Brushing teeth
   - Looking someone in the eye and saying "Hello".

By and large, it is the Stop behaviours that provoke the most intense frustration from parents and cause the most disruption.

Many parents take for granted that any time spent in the company of their children or teens will be punctuated by numerous instances of minor but irritating Stop and Start behaviour. Each of these minor behaviours, when viewed on its own, may not seem too terrible, but parents know that these behaviours do not usually occur singly. They come in clusters, and they add up quickly, wearing away at our good humour and good will.

Misbehaviour is usually considered to be typical and normal, just part of what loving parents have to put up with. We know that all children misbehave some of the time, and that some children misbehave a lot of the time. Many parents blame themselves for even feeling annoyed.

Often the annoyance comes from a growing realisation that most of this misbehaviour is not necessary, and it is certainly not beneficial to anyone, not for the parent or child. Parents can significantly alter, for the better, these behaviours.

Here is a list of behaviours that parents have told us they find most exasperating. The order in which I have listed them may not reflect the habits that concern you most. You will see that some of these actions may be deliberate, but a large number are the result of immaturity, impulsivity or habitual negative attention-seeking. You may not even consider some of these habits to be problematic; you may view them simply as childish characteristics that will fade away with maturity. But most parents do become frustrated and angry and may lash out, verbally or physically. Usually parents are very keen to reduce the number of Stop and Start behaviours they have to deal with.

1 Non-co-operation – the child is not doing as he has been told
2 Not following established rules and routines, i.e. the child regularly does things he has previously been told (numerous times!) not to do, and also does not do things he knows he should do
3 Sibling squabbles
4 Become easily upset when things do not go as he wants or expects
5 Tantrums
6 Acting helpless, giving up quickly, not wanting to try new things
7 Deliberate aggression or intimidation
8 Acting silly when not appropriate
9 Using language that parents disapprove of
10 Dawdling, getting distracted
11 Leaving things lying around instead of putting them back where they belong, not being willing to tidy them up
12 Interrupting
13 Boasting, showing off, misbehaving in public
14 Not saying "Please" and "Thank you"
15 Complaining about, avoiding or rushing carelessly through homework
16 Avoiding eye-contact
17 Asking many unnecessary questions
18 Telling parents what to do, correcting parents
19 Rarely playing by himself
20 Often asking for new toys
21 Too noisy: talking too loudly, running or shouting indoors, playing too wildly
22 Messy table manners
23 Poor personal hygiene
24 Chewing on clothes, fiddling, nose picking, etc.

25 Unintentionally being too rough or thoughtless (with people and belongings)

26 Lying

27 Stealing.

All of the behaviours on the list could be considered variations of Number 1 (non-co-operation) if the child continues to misbehave after the parent tells him not to. In a similar vein, most of the misbehaviours can be viewed as examples of Number 2 (not following rules and routines) because in most cases there already exists in the family a rule or guideline that addresses that misbehaviour.

Next follows a more in-depth explanation of the first three behaviours on the list. In order to dramatically reduce misbehaviour, we need to know exactly what we are up against.

1 NON-CO-OPERATION, i.e. not doing what the parent has asked the child to do, either in response to a Stop instruction or a Start instruction. Some typical Stop instructions might be:

- "Leave that alone."
- "Stop interrupting."
- "Let go."
- "Lower your voice."

These are typical Start instructions:

- "Write neatly."
- "Rinse all the soap out."
- "Hurry up."
- "Time to do your homework."

The non-co-operation can be expressed either verbally or non-verbally.

1a Verbal expressions of non-co-operation

Parents often call this: disrespect, answering back, back talk, rudeness, lip, being a smart-Alec or "not taking no for an answer".

These words summarise but do not really describe the disrespectful behaviour. What does the unco-operative child actually say? The child may:

- Argue and contradict
    "But you let him do it."
    "You said I could."
    "It's not my turn."

- Beg, plead, repeat, badger
    "Please, please, I really want to."
    "Do I really have to?"

- Insult (including calling parents names and swearing)
    "That's so stupid."
    "You're a mean mummy." (or worse)
    "You're the strictest dad in the world."

- Lie
    "Dad said it was O.K."
    "I wasn't."
    "I already did."
    "You never let me sit there."

- Trivialise
    "What's the big deal?"
    "I was only looking at it."
    "Whatever."

- Threaten
    "I don't love you any more."
    "I'm going to run away from home."

- Bribe, bargain
    "I'll put my toys away if you help me."
    "If you let me watch that programme, I'll do my revision as soon as
        it's over."

- Ask questions that are not a genuine request for information
    "Why can't I?"

- Delay
    "In a minute."
    "As soon as this programme is over."
    "I promise I'll do it."

- Justify, make excuses
    "I forgot."
    "I don't know how."
    "He did it first."

- Complain, blame, act like a victim, emotional blackmail
    "You're always picking on me."
    "I'm not your slave."
    "You love her best."

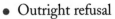

- Outright refusal
  "No."
  "You can't make me."

Any of the above can be made more infuriating by the addition of:

- A whiney, complaining, put-upon tone of voice
- Sarcasm
- Rolling of the eyes
- Crying, shouting, screaming
- Pouting and sulking
- Rude or silly faces or gestures or noises.

1b Non-verbal non-co-operation

This can take many forms:

- Ignoring, i.e. the child pretends he has not heard the instruction
- Crying, with no words
- The child looks at the parent, often with a mischievous smile, and continues with the misbehaviour
- The child runs away
- The child reacts aggressively, by hitting, pushing, kicking, etc.

1c There is an additional subset of quite subtle non-co-operation

- The child complies very, very slowly, or he does the objectionable action a few more times before stopping.
- The child complies only as long as the parent is watching, but reverts to the misbehaviour as soon as the parents' attention is elsewhere.
- The child obeys the "letter of the law" but disobeys the "spirit of the law". For example, if he is asked not to bang his fork on the table, he may bang his fork on his cup instead.
- The child complies partially. For example, if asked not to bang his fork on the table, he may continue to bang it on the table, but not so loudly
- The child follows the instruction but immediately does something else that is designed to annoy or provoke.

2 DOES NOT FOLLOW ESTABLISHED RULES AND

ROUTINES, i.e. the child does things he has been told many times not to do, and he regularly does not do things he knows he should do.

Examples:

- Plays with parents' or siblings' special possessions
- Stays in bed after the alarm
- Leaves his homework diary at school
- Splashes water onto the floor at bath time
- Wipes his mouth on his sleeve
- Goes into the road to retrieve a ball
- Wanders off by himself in shops
- Is physically aggressive with siblings
- Lies
- Takes money that he finds lying around
- Plays with knives or matches.

Parents often say about this child:

- "He can't be trusted".
- "I can't leave him alone for two minutes."
- "He should know better."
- "He lives in his own little world."
- "He does it on purpose."
- "He's so inconsiderate/selfish/thoughtless/immature."

When reminded of the rule or routine this child may:

- Very reluctantly comply, but only after much arguing, pleading for special exceptions, trying to bargain or to "bend" the rules
- Comply quickly and cheerfully (and possibly even apologise for having forgotten). But meanwhile he has "got away with" ignoring the parent's expectations until the parent notices and says something about it.

How deliberate is this disregard for established rules and routines? It can vary:

- The child may have genuinely forgotten what is expected of him, for a variety of possible reasons, which I will explore in the next chapter
- The child may remember but pretend to have forgotten the expectations
- He may sneak or hide, which clearly shows that he knows what behaviour is expected of him.

In the next chapters I will discuss why children deliberately ignore or flout known rules and routines, and what parents can do to reverse this behaviour.

3 SIBLING SQUABBLES, including:

- Grabbing, not taking turns, interrupting each other, reluctance to share
- Arguing about who gets the first, the most, the best, the front seat, the lap at story time, etc.
- Shrieking, screaming at each other
- Unintentionally being too rough: pushing and snatching
- Physical fights: hitting, pulling hair, biting, kicking, etc.
- Telling tales, complaining about the sibling to a parent, crying
- Finding fault, teasing, insulting, calling names, laughing at or deliberately annoying the other sibling
- Ignoring the other sibling.

Usually the older child is the stronger one, and will use his physical superiority, or the threat of it, to upset and annoy. The younger child soon learns to be wily; he becomes an expert at subtle winding up. The younger child annoys and provokes the older one. The older child retaliates, and the younger child cries or "tells". The older is blamed and scolded; the younger is rescued and comforted. The older child then resents the younger even more, and the younger child's victim role is further reinforced. A vicious circle develops, where no one wins. Over time, the younger child may adopt the unpleasant tactics of the older child.

Even when parents learn effective discipline strategies, a *small* amount of sibling squabbling will remain because a small amount is natural, inevitable and healthy. Sibling interactions are an arena in which children learn about peer relationships and about their impact on others.

For several generations now, ever since Freud started influencing our way of viewing families, it has been widely accepted that siblings quarrel and squabble because of deep, painful, unavoidable problems: rivalry, jealousy, envy, feelings of deprivation, etc. However, I have noticed that most sibling problems are caused by, and reinforced by, what parents do and how they do it, what parents say and how they say it. Simply put: parents' habits of blaming and rescuing are the cause of most sibling squabbles.

The techniques described in this book will significantly reduce the unpleasant interactions between siblings.

SECTION II The New Ways

Chapter 7

Why children misbehave and what parents can do about it

A certain amount of misbehaviour is a normal part of childhood. Some children misbehave a lot, and some misbehave very little, and it is essential to examine the reasons behind this before moving on to possible solutions. When we have a clear idea of why these differences exist, we can use our understanding to make changes to:

- Routines and rules
- What we say and how we say it
- What we do and how we do it.

We can create a more nearly optimal environment, one in which our children will be more and more able and willing to do the right thing.

For more than twenty years, scientists have been studying the observable differences between babies and children in order to identify and classify their characteristics and to attempt to distinguish the impact of genetics as separate from the impact of the environment.

Each child's genetic make-up is a combination of the characteristics that he shares with the rest of the human race plus those that he has inherited from his family. A child's environment is a combination of pre-natal experiences, his birth experience and his environment after birth. This includes the way his parents talk to him and touch him, the amount and quality of the food he is given, his experiences at school and with his peers, even subtle factors such as the level of background noise in his home, the cigarette smoke and exhaust fumes he is exposed to and how much time he spends out-of-doors.

The researchers have found that all the reasons for children's behaviour and misbehaviour boil down to an interplay of these factors:

A Human nature: Children are by definition less mature than adults. Their efforts to meet their needs are immature and often misguided. And children do not all mature at the same rate. A child's developmental stage (sometimes called "maturation age") is a much more significant influence on his behaviour than his chronological age is.

B Individual genetic inheritance: As we know, children are not all the same. Even siblings are very different from each other. Some children have extremes of inborn temperament, which drive them to behave, or misbehave, in certain ways. A carefully thought-out environment can definitely modify these innate behavioural tendencies, but most parents do not know how to do this, so they end up, understandably, feeling frustrated and helpless.

C Environment: Children react to what parents say and do and to how parents say it and do it. Parental habits greatly influence children's habits.

A Human nature

The following reasons for misbehaviour all have to do with children just being children. We cannot change these factors, so we need to take them into account and "work around" them.

1 Some annoying behaviour is, unfortunately, "horribly normal". It is perfectly appropriate for your child's age and developmental stage, so it cannot properly be termed misbehaviour. It is, however, possible to gently but firmly influence your child to give up certain annoying behaviours sooner than he might otherwise if he were simply left to his own devices. It is possible to help a child move more quickly towards a more mature developmental stage. A few examples are: running indoors, grabbing, interrupting, ignoring parents' instructions, dependence on a security blanket, bottle, dummy or other comfort object.

2 Young children are egocentric, almost totally concerned with their own wants and needs. Even if we explain and re-explain why they should wash their hands before dinner or hold our hand crossing the road, our reasons don't penetrate very far. The child may understand at the moment, but he often does not have the maturity to remember or even to care all that much. This is why explaining and lecturing and complaining get us nowhere. What does work is motivating your child to want to do the right thing and making it easier for him to do the right thing than to do the wrong thing.

3 We need to recognise that children have a different agenda from ours. A lot of the time we are thinking about what needs to get done next, while our children are thinking about playing and exploring. Children live in the moment and become very absorbed in whatever they are doing. It is essential to get their full attention before we give an instruction; otherwise they may hardly even hear us.

4 Immature human beings also have a different tempo from that of adults. They are often quite unaware of the passage of time, and they certainly do not understand the importance (to us) of time. They want what they want when they want it, which is usually right now! If we talk to children as if they understand or care about time (e.g. "Hurry up, we'll be late," "Come *on*, its 8 o'clock already"), we will make them and ourselves frustrated and resentful. We need to make the time in our busy days for children to be children: to do what is asked of them at a pace that is natural and comfortable for them. This is sometimes called, "Living at the speed of life, not at the speed of light".

5 We may be expecting the child to make a transition that is too abrupt for his developmental stage. It takes more time than we realise for the child's young brain to disengage from one activity or thought and to shift focus to the next. When we build in enough time for transitions, the child will be more willing, and we will find that we are saving time.

6 It is difficult for children (and even for many of us adults!) to sustain attention for a task that is not of their own choosing. They are not motivated from within to pursue that activity. *We*, the adults, need to provide the necessary motivation and incentive until the good habits are established.

7 Children are naturally enthusiastic and curious. They have a strong sense of adventure, and they love to explore. Often the impulse to explore is so strong that the child forgets all about, or even deliberately disregards, well-understood rules and instructions. The child may feel very frustrated and angry when he is told (or made) to stop doing what he has such a strong urge to do. This frustration can lead to whingeing, tantrums, dawdling, irritability, and disobedience, even deliberately winding up his parents. We need to give children appropriate outlets for this very healthy, very important need to explore.

8 When children are very anxious or worried, for whatever reason (for example: about school, peer relationships, sibling rivalry, parents fighting) they naturally become pre-occupied with securing their own comfort, which could be certain toys, certain routines, even certain behaviours. They are no longer thinking much about what is the right thing to do or about how to please the important adults in their lives. You could say that they go into survival mode. We need to identify, address and either eliminate or significantly reduce our children's worries if we want them to behave better.

B Individual genetic inheritance

For the past 75 years or so, due to the influence of Freud and our better understanding of psychological motivation, many people have assumed that children are the way they are solely due to their upbringing. Common sense tells us, however, that there must be more to it than that because different children in the same family, raised in a very similar way, have very different temperaments and develop very differently. Also, temperament differences are discernible within the first three months of life, long before the environment has been able to play much of a role in shaping the child's responses.

A minority of children misbehave a lot of the time. They cause their parents and teachers untold heartache and worry, as well as much exasperation and frayed nerves. This group of children has usually been problematic in one way or another since toddlerhood, often even since infancy (colic, excessive grizzling, disrupted sleeping, etc.). These are often the children who have a particular **extreme of inborn temperament**. It is often difficult for parents and teachers to realise how much a child's inborn temperament can influence his actions and reactions.

Some people would prefer to attribute early differences in temperament to environment rather than to inborn tendencies. For these people, it seems too pessimistic to accept that genetics play a large part in determining behaviour and reactions throughout a person's lifetime. The good news is that the researchers, although obviously unable to quantify it accurately, have reached the conclusion that genetic inheritance and environment probably each contribute approximately 50 percent to how someone "turns out". This means that a person will probably always have a tendency to react in a particular way, but that this tendency can be greatly modified or reinforced by environmental influences.

Scientists have exhaustively studied inborn differences, and new data continues to be generated. A number of distinct variables have been isolated which describe every child's innate tendencies to respond in certain ways to his surroundings. These tendencies are neurologically hard-wired into the infant's brain long before birth.

To summarise, these are the variables which have been pinpointed:

1 Activity level
2 Focus vs. distractibility and impulsivity
3 Adaptability vs. rigidity
4 Initial withdrawal vs. willingness to engage
5 Intensity (degree of reaction)

6 Sensitivity

7 Persistent mood (negative or positive)

8 Fine-motor skills (maturity vs. immaturity)

9 Regularity vs. irregularity.

Research into these variables has identified four distinct temperament types, which lie along a continuum:

1 Most of us have temperaments that fall roughly in the **middle** of the continuum. We are not given to extreme reactions (although a person who has experienced a great deal of stress may react in extreme ways).

2 Towards one end of the continuum we find what the researchers labelled the "**easy-to-raise**" child. This child's inborn temperament is relatively even and calm. This is the easy-going, "good natured" child who behaves well most of the time, even though he (or more often she) may have plenty of environmental reasons to misbehave. Only a very few children seem to be always sunny, willing, self-reliant and helpful, even in the face of adverse circumstances. These children do not get shouted at much or smacked.

3 Towards the other end of the continuum, we see the "**difficult-to-raise**" child. This child misbehaves more frequently. He demonstrates both the minor, irritating misbehaviours such as arguing back, whingeing and negative attention-seeking, as well as the bigger, more worrying misbehaviours such as lying, hitting and stealing. The exasperating characteristics of this temperament type provoke ever more parental criticism, telling off, lecturing, shouting, etc. This is the child who is most likely to get smacked, physically or verbally.

4 The fourth temperament type is often called the "**slow-to-warm-up**" or the "**quiet**" child. This child has some of the characteristics of the "difficult" child and some of the more average child. With careful handling his behaviour can be reined in, away from the "difficult" end.

These labels were those commonly used by the parents who were interviewed. Indirectly, these labels also describe the child's experience of his world. The "difficult-to-raise" child typically receives a lot of criticism and nagging, both at home and at school, which gradually eats away at his self-esteem and confidence. Children who are born with this extreme temperament can easily become "addicted" to their negative behaviour and to the negative attention it elicits from their parents and teachers. Life definitely feels more difficult for the difficult-to-raise child.

The implications of the different temperaments

Many of these difficult-to-raise and slow-to-warm-up children develop school problems, academic as well as behavioural and social, ranging from very mild to severe. They typically have problems with a number of the skills needed for school success: sitting still, staying quiet, paying attention, waiting patiently, remembering what the teacher has said, getting down to work quickly, staying focused on the task, paying careful attention to details, following rules and routines, delaying gratification, sharing, taking turns and accepting the authority of the adult.

Academically, they characteristically present with a "spiky profile" of cognitive (i.e. thinking) abilities. The highs may be very high, which often leads to predictions of above-average attainment. But the highs are often offset by some disconcertingly low cognitive scores. When professionals make the mistake of averaging out these high and low scores they end up with a very misleading result: the child's abilities appear to be comfortably within the normal range. This is a child who suffers from "subtle specific learning difficulties", and I do mean that he suffers. He can see that he is at least as bright as his peers are, so he cannot understand why school is such a struggle and a torment. Parents and teachers may inadvertently make matters worse by exhorting him to "try harder": study longer, listen more carefully, slow down, and pay closer attention. Every once in a while this child will surprise us, and even himself, by pulling it all together, behaviourally or academically, when there is a powerful and short-term extrinsic motivation, for example in order to be allowed to go on the school trip next week. But he is emotionally immature for his age; he has not yet developed the ability to motivate himself, so the occasional one or two steps forward are usually followed by a disappointing slide backwards.

The child whose inborn temperament falls towards the difficult-to-raise or slow-to-warm-up end of the continuum has been described by many names:

strong-willed	intense
explosive	fragile
chronically inflexible	out-of-sync
over-reactive	troubled
habitually non-compliant	off the rails
immature	
rebellious	
highly-strung	
sensitive	

And more recently many of these children have been given the labels of Attention Deficit Disorder, Oppositional-Defiant Disorder and Conduct Disorder.

The slow-to-warm up child and the difficult-to-raise child share a number of characteristics. Both have problems with impulsivity, distractibility and fine-motor skills, but the difficult-to-raise child has a much higher activity level so he gets into much more trouble.

Both adapt to changes and transitions slowly. The slow-to-warm-up child may react with anxiety and avoidance, while the difficult child reacts with anger and refusal.

Both of these extreme temperament types exhibit initial withdrawal. The difficult-to-raise child says, "No, I won't", whereas the slow-to-warm-up child responds with "I can't" or "It's too hard". Both often feel uncomfortable in unfamiliar surroundings and with new people, even if a parent is present. The slow-to-warm-up child may withdraw into sucking his thumb, clinging to a parent, whingeing or crying, resisting instructions to "act his age". He may become an expert at making excuses that get him out of uncomfortable situations and activities. The difficult child is more likely to react with negative attention-seeking and testing. The slow-to-warm-up child often shares the hypersensitivity, irregularity and negative mood of the difficult-to-raise child, but his reactions are, on the whole, significantly less intense. Even when the slow-to-warm-up child feels an emotion strongly, it is not very obvious, even to people who know the child well. He may be seen as a dawdler, a daydreamer and a "cry-baby", he may be thought careless and possibly even "a bit dim" or "slow". Although his behaviour can be quite frustrating, the slow-to-warm-up child is rarely accused of deliberate misbehaviour. Instead, he may be perceived as immature, self-absorbed or eccentric, lacking self-esteem, lazy, possibly even depressed.

When I talk to parents and teachers about the characteristics of a child who has a difficult temperament or is the slow-to-warm-up type, I often hear this refrain:

"I understand that some children really can't help themselves. But my child (or pupil) can do the right thing if he wants to. When he makes the effort, he can pay attention (or write neatly, or spell properly, or sit still, or control his anger, etc.). But he just can't be bothered most of the time. And I am sure that sometimes he does the wrong thing just to wind me up!"

And there is some validity to this viewpoint. What often happens is this:

- The child starts out with a genuine difficulty.
- He gets criticised repeatedly by parents and teachers who do not realise that the child is just doing what comes naturally for *him*.
- He gives up trying. This is called having a "bad attitude".
- He gets criticised even more.
- He drifts into the habit of negative attention-seeking.
- He gets criticised even more.
- Eventually, out of anger or despair, he fights back. In revenge mode, he does the wrong thing on purpose. He gets a kick out of making parents and teachers angry or upset.

There is a distinct set of relative strengths that often go hand-in-hand with both the slow-to-warm-up temperament and the difficult temperament. These children are often creative and inventive. They are often quirky, lateral thinkers. When channelled constructively, this ability can be a huge asset and can bring them much satisfaction as well as respect from their peers. But unharnessed it can easily turn into a liability. We are all familiar with the "class clown" who has a ready wit and can disrupt any lesson. This child may have considerable innate musical or sports talent but lack the inner motivation to keep practising. So he is frequently nagged to slow down and pay attention, to do his best or to correct his mistakes. Due to their impulsivity and immaturity, these children simply cannot be expected to motivate themselves. Another characteristic is their love of extremes, their daredevil sense of adventure. Unchecked, it can easily lead them astray. But with some thought and planning, parents and teachers can inject excitement into even mundane tasks and subject matter.

By and large, children with problematic temperaments tend to be visual thinkers with good spatial and holistic abilities. They are much weaker at understanding and remembering information that is sequential and verbally presented. Many of these children exhibit an innocence and an idealism that is refreshing when it is not infuriating.

C Environment

What parents and teachers do and don't do influences what children do and don't do. When we change what we do, children change what they do.

In the next few pages I will highlight some of the common causes of family problems and give a brief indication of how they can be resolved. The remainder of the book expands on the key skills which will help you achieve a calmer, easier and happier family life.

1 Children are natural imitators, and the brighter they are, the more accurately they imitate.

2 Often the child has experienced that his parents will not notice whether he complies or not. And if we shout up the stairs or from another room, or if we fling commands over our shoulder as we are walking away, the child will not think that what we are saying is important. In both cases, the solution is the same. We need to be there both physically and mentally, in order for our children to take us seriously.

3 If we often sound impatient or annoyed or critical when we are talking to our children they will not be motivated to try to please us. We need to cultivate a polite tone of voice.

4 Our instruction may seem to the child to be merely a request, an observation or a suggestion, rather than something that he really has to do and do it now. The child may mistakenly be led to believe that we are giving him a choice when we start sentences with wishy-washy phrases like:

- "Let's…"
- "How about…"
- "I wish you would…"
- "You forgot to…"
- "Would you like …"

Similarly, when we use a tentative tone of voice, or tag an "O.K.?" onto the end of the sentence, we unwittingly turn our instruction into a request. The child will feel perfectly within his rights to reply, "No, I don't want to". We need to make it clear that we are telling, not suggesting, both by the words we use and by our calm, firm tone of voice.

- "Now it's time for you to …"
- "Now you need to …"

5 When we drift into the habit of repeating ourselves, children will tune us out, waiting subconsciously for the repeated reminders. Only when the parent is about to blow a gasket will the children take the instruction seriously. If we are willing to repeat an instruction five times, we will soon find that we "need" to repeat it five times. Chapters 12, 13 and 14 explain how to teach children to pay attention the first time.

6 In addition to their ordinary curiosity about the world, children have a special kind of curiosity, a strong need to make sense of their world, and in particular of their relationships. They ask themselves:

- Who decides what happens – me or Mum or Dad or my teacher?
- Do Mum and Dad mean what they say?
- Is this just a rule for home or also for the supermarket?
- Will my parents follow-through and make me do things?
- Or will they tell me off but eventually give in?

As with most annoying behaviour, often it is the child with a naturally sensitive, intense, impulsive temperament who will challenge the parents' limits and reactions more often than the more easy-going child will.

7 If we have not been consistent about following through on our rules and instructions in the past, the child will not assume that we really mean it this time. So he will just wait and see what happens, which buys him more time to do what he feels like doing. This is called "testing". Even children who are usually co-operative will test in situations where they sense, from the parents' initial reaction, that parents are uncomfortable about following through. They may "bend the rules" without quite breaking them.

The "normal" amount of inconsistency is often too much for the sensitive, intense, impulsive child to handle. His easy-going sibling may be able to adapt to changes and "go with the flow", but the difficult-to-raise child and the slow-to-warm-up child do not have this ability. Lack of consistency can occur for many reasons:

- Parents are focused on being "fair" and flexible and trying to make their children happy. Parents are confusing what children *need* with what children *want*. Parents give children the scope to make choices that children do not yet have the maturity to handle.
- Parents keep hoping that potentially explosive situations will somehow defuse themselves.
- Out of guilt, or for a "quiet life", parents give in when children whinge, nag, scream or refuse.
- Out of love or a sense of duty, parents do too much for their children, not realising that what children need is training in self-reliance.
- Parents prefer a spontaneous life-style themselves and do not realise how important routines are for children, especially those children with characteristics at the "difficult" end of the spectrum. The parents make up the rules as they go along.

Regardless of our reasons, we need to put a lot of effort into being consistent, even though it may result in inconvenience to ourselves.

8 Unfortunately, our modern life-style does not bring out the best in children – or in ourselves! There are numerous aspects of modern life that combine to make children over-stimulated, less motivated to co-operate, less interested in doing their best or in thinking sensibly. Some of the life-style issues which are influential in winding our children up to misbehave are:

 – too much time spent in front of a screen
 – too much background noise and not enough silence
 – too many toys and treats
 – being entertained too much of the time, with not enough time set aside for children to learn to occupy themselves creatively
 – having too much done for them, not being required to join in with housework, meal preparation, errands, pet care
 – too much rushing ("Hurry up." "Come on." "Let's go." "We'll be late.")
 – too much junk food
 – not enough exercise
 – not enough close supervision of homework and revision
 – not enough good-quality sleep
 – not enough exposure to beauty and to nature.

Parents need to be in charge of the decision-making to prevent children drifting into unproductive, unwholesome habits. Being in charge means deciding what we want for our family and being willing to do what it takes to achieve that. You may feel overwhelmed at the thought of making lifestyle changes, especially if there are problems with quite a few issues. However, there are skills that can help you to do this. For example, once you know how to give an instruction that your children will follow, you can make all the important changes. Chapters 12, 13 and 14 show you how to achieve co-operation.

9 Depending on the extent of the negativity in the household, for example repeating and reminding, criticising, threatening, contradicting, blaming, shouting, and also depending on the child's inborn temperament, the child may become very frustrated, resentful and angry and may be tempted to retaliate. Such children are motivated by a feeling of revenge. They feel they have been treated unfairly, and they deliberately set out to make life just as miserable for their parents and siblings and sometimes for their teachers as well.

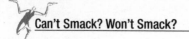

They become experts at annoying and upsetting the grown-ups. We can reduce and eventually eliminate this resentment by learning to stay calm and friendly.

10 When a child believes that he cannot perform a task to the parent's or teacher's satisfaction, he may avoid doing it. He would rather get into trouble for disobeying and be thought bad, than get into trouble for doing it poorly and be thought stupid or clumsy. Therefore we need to make sure that a child can easily do what we ask of him. And if he cannot, we need to teach him how.

11 If a child receives a lot of criticism and nagging, and is often spoken to in an impatient, annoyed manner, he may come to see himself as bad or naughty, the troublemaker, the one nobody likes. This becomes his identity. The child who thinks of himself as bad no longer even bothers to try and please his parents. He has given up. He does not think it is possible to get positive attention from adults. He may even think that he cannot possibly ever learn to be "good" in future. When he does try to co-operate, his efforts are often poor or go unnoticed. This child may even seem proud of his identity as the bad one: "I can't be good, but I can be the best at being bad". But underneath the bravado, this child is angry and anxious, sometimes blaming himself, sometimes blaming others. This negative attitude can change when parents change. We need to show our child that he can please us. See Chapters 9, 10 and 11.

12 The child who does not feel successful at school, academically or socially, is often, as a result, irritable, angry, anxious, ashamed, spending a lot of time trying not to be found out, blaming himself or others. We sometimes forget that school is a child's "job". Children, like adults, define themselves largely through their job. As adults, if we feel unsuccessful at our job, we have the option of changing jobs or even changing careers altogether. Rarely does a child or teenager have these choices. So children who feel unsuccessful suffer. They may suffer in silence, pretending nothing is wrong, or they may suffer noisily, making problems for everyone. Either way, lack of success takes a heavy toll on their self-esteem, and these children become less and less willing to co-operate, less and less interested in following rules and routines, less and less pleasant to be with. The suffering is real, whatever the reasons are for the lack of school success. When children's educational needs are consistently met, they gradually become more confident, even those children with specific learning difficulties.

13 Sibling jealousy and rivalry are strong emotions that can drive children to misbehave, particularly when parents' reactions to squabbling lead to negative attention-seeking. Each child needs frequent one-to-one "Quality Time" with a parent. This will improve the family atmosphere very rapidly.

14 Children have a natural developmental drive to make choices about things in their lives that matter to them. Like adults, they need to be able to make things happen. We all need to exercise some control, power and autonomy over important aspects of our lives.

Of course, there are many times each day when we, the parents, must make decisions for our children because we know that they have not yet developed the maturity to make a sensible choice. Children think they *need* whatever they *want*. We know that needs and wants often do not bear even a passing resemblance to each other.

However, it is easy for busy parents to fall into the habit of making decisions for our children in matters where they are equipped to decide for themselves. We often say, "Wear your jumper, it's chilly", when we could just as easily make the same point by asking, "Do you want to wear your jumper or just take it?" We tend to order, "Drink your juice, we're late", when we could ask, "Do you want a full glass of juice or half a glass?"

To children, it often seems as if we are bossing them around all day long. That is partly a result of each instruction being repeated several times because the busy, stressed parent did not first get the child's attention and did not stay and wait for the child to comply. We also unintentionally annoy children by telling them to do things that they would have done anyway, if we had forced ourselves to be patient and wait just a few seconds longer.

When children are not allowed to exercise their normal drive to make developmentally appropriate choices, they often feel unappreciated, unheard, unseen, disapproved of and powerless. A battle for power can develop. The child wants to be boss, and one sure-fire way for children to feel powerful and gain attention is to not co-operate. When parents react to non-co-operation by arguing back, shouting, or even smacking, the child feels powerful; he feels he is in control. He has the satisfaction of having made you lose your cool. The solution to this problem is to avoid all unnecessary instructions. In areas where your child has shown good judgment, allow him to make decisions, rather than doing his thinking for him.

15 Sometimes a child who is reasonably co-operative at home will act up in the presence of other children (his own age or older or younger). He is attempting to prove that he is not weak or "sad" or a goody-goody or a mummy's boy. There is a growing culture, particularly among boys, of respect and admiration for aggression, meanness, and contempt. So the misbehaving child tries to "buy" high status by being unpleasant. This child may be easily influenced by others because his basic human need for acceptance, appreciation and approval is not being met. The more this basic need is met by his parents and teachers, the less he will need to look for confirmation of his worth amongst his peers.

16 Lack of time alone with each parent. Every child and every teenager *needs* to spend time alone with each parent. It is as strong a need as the need for food or water. Without siblings present, the child can relax more, and usually the parent can too! Of course, a family needs to spend enjoyable time together as a complete unit. But each child also needs to frequently experience the one-to-one bonding that occurs when each parent demonstrates, by setting aside time for that child alone, that this child is liked and valued, as well as loved. The quality time needs to be frequent and predictable, doing something that the parent and the child both enjoy (not in front of a screen). It also needs to be labelled as such by the parent so that the child can see that the parent values this special time together.

One-to-one quality time helps the child *want* to co-operate. It also awakens in the child the desire to imitate the *positive* habits and qualities and values of that parent.

17 Attention-seeking

Parents and teachers often apply the phrase "attention-seeking" to particular children in a disparaging way, as if we believe that it is a bad thing to want so much attention. In fact, we are all "attention-seekers", but some children get hooked on doing negative things and getting negative attention.

Humans are seeking attention almost all of the time. We need attention, we thrive on attention, and we soon droop without attention. Most of us have learned how to get the kind of attention we like. We may do our work carefully; we may choose to act cheerfully even when we're feeling grumpy; we may tell amusing anecdotes; we may be particularly kind to our friends when they are going through a rough time; we may go out of our way to do a favour for someone whom we know will be appreciative.

The attention we all want and need is appreciation of our strengths, acceptance of our frailties and approval of our efforts. Children need this kind of attention even more than we adults do. We have learned, to some degree, how to give ourselves some of the appreciation, acceptance and approval that we need. Children have not yet learned how to give themselves this positive attention, so they depend on us to provide them with it, just as they depend on us for food, clothing and shelter.

We can easily understand that when a child's pleasant, co-operative behaviour is met with a lot of appreciation and approval then the child will naturally be motivated to do those actions again. But that's not what usually happens. Desperate parents of difficult children ask: "*Why doesn't my child realise that he would get plenty of positive attention if he just co-operated and were nicer to be around?*" The answer, unfortunately, is because it's not usually true! In even the most loving households, children usually get more attention for misbehaving than for behaving well. Parents often forget to notice or to appreciate a child for simply doing what he was told to do or for following the rules and routines. We mostly notice and respond to the problems.

What happens when a child's unpleasant, unco-operative behaviour receives a lot of criticism, complaints, reminders and lectures while the positive behaviour goes largely unnoticed, taken for granted? Interestingly, these negative parental reactions *also* increase the likelihood of the misbehaviour happening again. If positive attention is thin on the ground, our children will, understandably, aim for the negative attention. From the child's point of view, any reaction is better than being ignored. Compared to being ignored, negative attention feels like love. After a while, some children get hooked on doing negative things and getting negative attention. The vicious circle can become habitual for both the parents and for the child. What are some of the things children do when they are seeking negative attention? The perennial favourites are:

- Doing the opposite of what they are told
- Tantrums
- Showing off
- Baby talk
- Swearing
- Acting helpless
- Sibling squabbles
- Endless unnecessary questions

- Interrupting
- Whingeing, arguing and complaining
- Dawdling.

Occasionally the negative attention-seeking is deliberate and quite conscious. That is why explaining and lecturing do not usually get us the results we want. But more often, the child will remain oblivious to the reasons for his misbehaviour. The negative attention-seeking has become habitual and unconscious, and the child does not understand why he does it or even realise he is doing it.

Once again, it is the children who were born with an extreme temperament type who most easily become "addicted" to negative behaviour and to the negative responses it elicits from parents, teachers and even siblings. As simplistic as this may sound, the solution to negative attention-seeking is to keep noticing and mentioning their acceptable behaviour. Chapters 9, 10 and 11 explain in great detail how to do this.

18 When we have drifted into the habit of repeating and reminding our children a lot, and they have therefore developed the habit of not listening and not taking us seriously, we become, understandably, easily irritated, possibly even resentful. We find that we have a short fuse. We may not scream or slap, but we forget to smile. We forget to have fun with our children. Not surprisingly, our children may feel burdened and weighed down by our subtle negativity. This book is full of strategies that can help you enjoy your children again.

Regardless of which of the above causes of misbehaviour initially applied to your child, chronic lack of co-operation is, in a sense, a cry for help. This child is telling us that his life is not working right. There is not enough of what he needs in order to thrive, and too much of what he definitely does not need.

Chapter 8
What behaviour is achievable with the new ways

What parents want

Parents often say, "*I just want my child to be happy*". This is an understandable sentiment, but unfortunately it can gradually lead families down a slippery slope that ends in martyrdom and irritation for the parents and brattishness and ingratitude in the child. Why? When we set out to make our children happy, we find ourselves catering to what they know they want, rather than to what we believe they need. Wants and needs often have very little in common. Children who get too much of what they want (more videos, more fast food, more toys, later bedtimes, etc.) and not enough of what they need (earlier bedtimes, more vegetables, consistent routines, time alone with each parent, etc.) are no fun to live with. The irony inherent in trying to make our children happy is that it so often results in the very opposite: unsatisfied, unconfident, unmotivated children who do not even value all the possessions they have. And of course, parents living with these irritable, petulant children aren't too happy either.

Instead, parents need to identify which personal characteristics children need to develop to be able to *help themselves* become happier. Note that in that last sentence, I did not write that certain characteristics could *make* our children happy, only that they would *help* our children to be happier. And I wrote *happier*, not *happy*. There are no absolutes when it comes to humans; we are just too complex. We can aim for and achieve a calmer, easier, happier life for ourselves and for our children, but life will never be just plain calm, easy and happy. Let's let go of the myth of happiness as a pure, unadulterated, sustainable emotion. Let's rule out the unattainable "happiness" as a goal, and aim for the definitely attainable "calmer, easier, happier".

Children who like themselves

Children who like themselves like to behave themselves. Interestingly, the reverse is also true: children who learn to behave themselves learn to like themselves. One of our goals as parents is to help our children feel good about themselves: competent, confident and self-respecting. Another parental goal is maximising co-operation and reducing conflict and stress.

These goals are especially important to keep in mind for children with subtle specific learning difficulties or intense temperaments because these children often experience more than their fair share of anxiety, frustration, anger, embarrassment, confusion and despair. They deserve to feel good about their abilities and efforts. And so do their parents!

Perhaps you have felt discouraged, in the past, when you saw that your children seemed to lack the co-operation, self-confidence and self-discipline necessary to enable them to take risks, to set goals, to work diligently towards goals, etc. As parents, every day we are creating an environment in which our children learn about themselves and the world. We have a choice about what environment we choose to create. We can choose to create a new environment! When we change the way we habitually relate to our children, they will automatically begin to see themselves differently and behave differently. Therefore we do not need to try to change our children. We need to change our own responses and habits.

It is never too late to change our own unproductive or unpleasant habits. As we change our habits, the children will change their habits. It is never too late to change how a child views himself. Let's replace guilt about the past with determination about the future.

Habits that breed happier families

What are the qualities our children need to develop in order to help themselves to be happier? When I ask parents to think about this question, I usually hear some version of the following list:

1 Co-operation – Doing what a trusted adult tells them to do, the first time they are told, and without a fuss, *even when they do not feel like it.*

2 Confidence – Knowing and appreciating and using one's talents and abilities and strengths, knowing and accepting and being willing to improve one's weaknesses.

3 Motivation – The willingness to do, and to keep doing, all the steps needed to reach our goals, even though we may not intrinsically enjoy doing those steps. (Homework, brushing teeth, walking the dog, violin practice and saving money are all examples of actions that often require motivation to overcome reluctance or resistance.)

4 Self-reliance – Doing for themselves everything that they are capable of doing, rather than expecting or hoping or waiting for someone else to do it for them.

5 Consideration – Caring about and understanding how one's actions
affect others.

These five qualities are the building blocks for a calmer, easier, happier life in
the present and in the future. These are the qualities that will help children
and teens to enjoy their families, make and keep friends, reach their potential
in school and eventually find satisfaction as adults in the areas of
relationships, careers and leisure pursuits.

These five qualities or characteristics are *not* inborn, although there is
mounting evidence that certain inborn temperament types have tendencies
towards or away from these characteristics.

These five qualities can be developed. They can become habits. And the
beauty of learning how to develop these habits in your children is that you
will be fulfilling two purposes: you will be influencing your children to show
more of their best sides *as they grow up*, and you will also be influencing them
to show more of their best sides *as adults*.

Of course, the next question parents always ask is: "How can we get our
children into the habits of being co-operative, confident, motivated, self-
reliant and considerate?"

At The New Learning Centre, we have found that one of these five habits is
the gateway into the other four habits. So rather than worrying about how
you are going to train your children in all five habits, you need to concentrate
most of your training focus on that one habit, and the other four will follow
quite easily and with much less effort.

Co-operation: The gateway habit

The child who is unco-operative does not stand much chance of developing
SELF-CONFIDENCE or strong self-esteem. How can he like himself
when he is the recipient of so much impatience and annoyance, when he
hears daily nagging, threats, blame, complaints, criticism, warnings and un-
asked for advice? The child who is often unco-operative is also often angry –
angry at his parents and teachers for always getting "on his case", angry at his
siblings and at other children who seem to be sailing through life, succeeding
where he is failing, and angry at himself for disappointing and upsetting the
important adults in his life. When children are trained in the habit of co-
operation, they naturally become more confident.

The child who is not yet in the habit of doing what he is told *even when he
doesn't feel like it* does not develop the impulse-control or self-discipline that

is needed for MOTIVATION. As all adults know, to achieve most goals and to complete most important projects, we have to "grasp the nettle" and tackle some mundane or tedious tasks. Motivation is the willingness to do and to keep doing those boring or difficult or even scary bits so that we can reach our goals and fulfil our plans.

Children who are not co-operative most of the time are also usually not SELF-RELIANT. Here is why: Co-operation can be defined, in a narrow sense, as doing what you are told. Self-reliance, however, goes an important step further. Self-reliance can be defined, rather simplistically, as telling yourself the right thing to do and then doing it. To get into the habit of doing the right things because he tells himself to, the child needs first to get into the habit of doing those things when he is told to. Only by doing those things repeatedly, because he has been told to, will a child eventually see *for himself* the benefit of doing them. But when the largely unco-operative child is told to tidy his room, or empty the dishwasher, or feed the cat, or walk the dog, or pack his PE kit, he does not co-operate! He often manages to avoid the task, either not doing it at all or else doing a messy, incomplete job of it. So he rarely practises doing properly all those little jobs that he is quite capable of doing properly, and he misses out on the satisfaction of a job well done. Plus, he continues to think that it is not *his* job, but his parents' job, to get him to do things.

The unco-operative, angry child is rarely CONSIDERATE. He often behaves very thoughtlessly and even aggressively, although his real nature, hidden beneath the pain and anger and bad habits, may be very caring and affectionate.

95% co-operation

Parents are entitled to co-operation about 95% of the time.

Children thrive best when they are co-operating 95% of the time.

Even sensitive, intense, impulsive children are capable of co-operating 95% of the time.

95% co-operation means that if you give your child 100 instructions per day (a low average, believe it or not!), your child will start to comply within a few seconds, without a fuss, to 95 or so of the instructions. With the remaining 5 instructions, your child, not being a robot, will probably not comply right away.

This book will teach you skills for achieving this 95% co-operation rate and will also teach you how to achieve compliance (although not so immediate) with the remaining 5%, so that you are less and less tempted to do what we all know doesn't work: repeat yourself, nag, complain, criticise, lecture, threaten, shout …. or smack. It is not difficult to achieve this calmer, easier, happier state of affairs when you practise these new skills until they become habitual.

This book can teach you new ways of communicating your expectations, rules and values. Parents tell us that it is like learning a new language: it can feel awkward and frustrating at first, but with fluency come confidence, pride and satisfaction.

Instead of smacking (physically or verbally), which is rarely effective and makes everyone feel bad, you will learn new ways of speaking that very quickly motivate children to try and do the right thing. Over time this significantly boosts their confidence and self-esteem.

This book can teach you how to help your child become more and more willing to do what you tell him to do, first time and without fuss, even when it is not what he feels like doing. This includes teaching your child to:

- Maintain a respectful tone of voice even when he is annoyed, disappointed or upset
- Say how he feels, rather than reacting with misbehaviour
- Make requests, rather than complaining or blaming
- Remember and follow the family routines and rules, so that you do not have to keep reminding and prompting. After all, this is one of the ultimate goals of parental discipline: to raise children who will tell *themselves* the right thing to do, rather than relying on someone else to do their thinking for them.

Our aim is to help children become more co-operative (and consequently also more confident, motivated, self-reliant and considerate) by helping them to *want* to co-operate.

By practising the Calmer, Easier, Happier Parenting methods, I guarantee that within two to four weeks you will see a definite improvement, and within two to four months you will see even more dramatic improvements in your child's behaviour.

As we know, life with children is made up of one small incident after another … after another … after another …! When we learn how to deal with each incident positively, firmly and consistently, our lives improve dramatically and so do our children's lives.

So how does this magical transformation take place within a few short months? When we look at the factors which determine behaviour, we can see that all but one of the factors are still the same. Obviously, human nature hasn't changed; your child's DNA is still exactly the same; he is still the same age (plus just a few months) and at almost the same developmental stage. The *only* thing that has changed is the child's environment, specifically what the parents are doing and saying differently. And this change in the parents' behaviour results in vastly improved behaviour and self-esteem of the children.

You will need to *keep practising* the Calmer, Easier, Happier Parenting Skills. For how long? Until your children leave home! The issues you are dealing with will keep evolving, of course. There will never come a day when you can safely say, "There! I've resolved all the issues once and for all, so I can go back to my old ways". And if you do drift back to your old habits, your children will sooner or later drift back to their old habits as well. Arguing, teasing siblings, messiness, ignoring you, lying, etc. – these will all creep back into daily family life.

A frequently asked question

Parents may worry at first:

"Training sounds like something you do to dogs! Children have a lot more intelligence than animals, not to mention a soul and a conscience. Surely we shouldn't just be training them to obey on command? I, for one, want my child to think for himself."

My reply:

This question raises several issues:

1 Training means developing habits. I find it amusing that sometimes people object to "training children as if they were dogs". The sad fact is that dogs are often treated better than children are! That is because we know that dogs cannot understand language, so we are not tempted, when we train them, to do what so obviously would not work: lecturing, criticising, reasoning, explaining, suggesting, bargaining, etc. Those techniques do not usually work with children either, but once a child starts to understand language, it is much harder for us to realise and remember that.

2 Dogs learn new habits largely through clear, consistent commands and consistent rewards. They learn to "behave appropriately", and as a result they rarely get smacked or shouted at. Do you remember what I said about how repeating, reminding, suggesting and criticising eat away at our children's self-esteem? Have you noticed that self-esteem is not a problem for most dogs?

3 I agree that we want our children to develop the habit of thinking for themselves and questioning what they see and hear. We want them to retain their individuality, their unique personality and their creativity. We do not want them to succumb to peer pressure and media manipulation. You will soon see that getting children into the habit of co-operation actually enhances their confidence, creativity and individuality. That is because children who do what they are told most of the time receive far more appreciation, approval and smiles, as well as more quality time from parents. This automatically encourages their best qualities to flourish.

4 If we are truthful, we do not want our children to question everything we say. We do not want them to automatically respond "Why?" or "Why do I have to?" as a whinge, as an argument, as a diversionary tactic, or as a way to wind us up. We do want our children to be curious, adventurous and to have enquiring minds, but we also want our children to respect us, to obey us and to trust that we have good reasons for what we expect of them. The word "obedience" has gone out of favour. But it is a good old-fashioned word for a very necessary habit: doing what they are told, *first time*, without a fuss, even when they don't feel like doing it.

Chapter 9

Descriptive Praise: What it is and why it is so effective at improving behaviour

Different kinds of praise

We are always coming across magazine articles that tell us to praise our children: "You're a great kid!" "You're so special to me." "You're the best!"

We assume that praising our children will help them to become more confident and to feel loved and secure and special: "You're such a good boy." "I'm so proud of you." "Good job!" "You make me so happy!"

We also praise our children to encourage them to try new activities that they might be anxious about or to not give up when the going gets tough: "You're doing really well!" "Keep up the good work!" "That's wonderful!" "Well done!" "That's amazing!"

We hope that our praise will motivate our children to do more of the activities that we have decided are good for them but that they do not want to do: "You're very talented." "You're so brave." "Aren't you clever!" "Brilliant!" "Super!"

Our goals here are good and important ones, but unfortunately we often use a form of praise that is not very effective. This type of vague, exaggerated praise is called *evaluative praise* because the adult is evaluating, passing judgment, saying or implying that the child is good.

For me, the proof that evaluative praise is not very effective is that most of the parents I meet lavish this form of praise on their children and yet still worry that their children lack confidence, feel insecure, or are not motivated to persevere with difficult tasks or to try their best.

You might be thinking that the only problem is that these children are not getting enough praise. But my experience shows me that this is not the case. Even children who get criticised a lot are also praised a lot because we all know it is what we should do. In fact, it is often the child in the family who gets told off the most who also gets praised the most. Guilt-ridden parents try to make up for their verbal and physical smacking by piling on the praise when they remember and when they feel up to it.

These are the reasons why evaluative praise does not accomplish what we want it to.

1 When just-O.K. behaviour or performance gets a response of "Terrific!", inflation soon sets in. Parents find themselves reaching for even stronger superlatives when they want to show they are *really* pleased or proud.

2 Parents say "Wonderful" and "Terrific" and "Great" automatically. The child can see that often the parent has barely glanced at the drawing, handstand or Lego™ construction.

3 The child can see that he is not amazing or wonderful compared to other children so he does not believe his parents' sweeping, over-the-top statements. The child may feel like a fake because he knows that the overblown generalities are not true. He can easily remember numerous instances of the exact opposite, when he was not good or clever or thoughtful or brave, etc.

4 In his own childish way, the child may be thinking: "My parents are the only ones who say I'm beautiful (or great at sports or clever or strong or talented). The rest of the world obviously doesn't agree with them. If my parents really do believe what they're telling me, they must have poor judgment or be deluded. I can't trust their view of me. And I can't trust them to understand my worries about not measuring up to their inflated view of me". When parents applaud a mediocre effort, the child wonders whether his parents assume he is not capable of doing any better.

5 And finally, evaluative praise is too general to convey any useful information to the child about what to do in the future to get more acknowledgement and appreciation.

However, what *does* work to achieve our aims is a new kind of praise called *Descriptive Praise*. This new "language" has the power to transform family life: improving the behaviour of the child and also of the parent, easing problematic relationships, restoring appreciation and confidence all around.

Descriptive Praise is a powerful motivator. It can gradually melt stubborn resistance and defiance, improve concentration and attention to detail, and motivate children and parents to be their best selves. This is a technique worth learning and practising *non-stop*, especially if you find yourself shouting, criticising, yanking or smacking more than you would like.

Simply stated, Descriptive Praise consists of noticing and mentioning *exactly* what your children have *done right* or what they have *not done wrong*.

In order to Descriptively Praise, parents need to momentarily stop everything they are doing and really pay attention to what the child is doing and not doing. The very act of slowing down and paying attention, in itself, gives us a valuable "window", a little bit of time that we can devote to communicating our love and appreciation.

Descriptive Praise is good for both the child and the parent. Most importantly, Descriptive Praise treats children with the respect they deserve, regardless of how annoying we may find their behaviour. Over time, Descriptive Praise raises the self-esteem and self-confidence of all children. It demonstrates to children that they are not just loved but also liked and approved of. A steady diet of Descriptive Praise gently nudges the child to continually redefine himself as more and more sensible, capable, loveable, respectful, considerate, etc. Over time, the difficult child becomes less angry and anxious and whingey around his parents, more relaxed and confident, because he is no longer expecting to be told off.

Descriptive Praise lets children know *exactly* what we want them to do and not do. It is a huge relief to children not to have to work out what exactly we mean when we say, "Behave!" By telling the child exactly what he did right (or did not do wrong), Descriptive Praise gives him a foolproof way to get even more positive attention. With this new kind of praise, children see and hear, many times a day, that their parents are pleased with them. This motivates them to try even more to do what is expected of them. Descriptive Praise proves to children that they can do the right thing, since they just did it. It therefore does not seem so difficult or objectionable to do it again. As children become more confident that they can behave well, they become more willing to think about their behaviour, rather than to react impulsively or defiantly. They start to realise for themselves what is sensible and what is not.

More effectively than any other technique I know, Descriptive Praise helps children to become much more co-operative and willing. Often it is the quest for parental approval that first motivates children to think about how they can get more Descriptive Praise by being more co-operative, more considerate, more helpful, etc. Over time this new positive behaviour becomes habitual. Eventually, children who have received a lot of Descriptive Praise choose positive behaviour because they have internalised our values. They notice for themselves that they feel better about themselves when their behaviour is in line with their values. This is the birth of conscience.

The benefits to parents of Descriptive Praise are immediate and enormous. Parents feel more relaxed and more confident as they see their children becoming visibly happier, calmer, more motivated to challenge themselves and more at ease in the world. One parent of a sensitive, intense, impulsive child told us, *"Now that I am using Descriptive Praise, I feel, finally, that I am a good mother"*.

Chapter 10
How to Descriptively Praise

The concept of Descriptive Praise is easy to grasp:

  a Notice what the child is doing right or at least O.K.-ish.

  b Tell the child exactly what you notice.

  c Leave out the evaluative praise.

But parents tell me again and again that it is not easy to remember to do it consistently. There are several reasons for this and more than one may apply to you:

1 When we are busy, rushing or stressed, we focus on getting things done which leaves no time for noticing our child's O.K. behaviour.

2 No matter where we grew up, most of us did not hear much Descriptive Praise, so it feels like a foreign language to us. We may feel awkward when we first start practising this new way of communicating.

3 You may be highly sceptical about the benefits I claim for Descriptive Praise. You may assume that nagging, criticising, shouting, and even the occasional smack are universally used to control behaviour. It is difficult to motivate yourself to try something new if you do not really think it will make much of a difference.

4 You may be blaming your children for their misbehaviour, forgetting that how children behave is a combination of three factors only: human nature, the child's inborn temperament, and what we do and say as parents. There is no logic in blaming our children for something that is clearly not their fault.

A reluctance to try new ways of doing things is a well-documented human characteristic. As you read on you will learn the strategies that other parents have used to help them remember to Descriptively Praise and to help them overcome the natural human resistance to change.

When we are rushing around trying to get things done, our mind's eye is on the next errand and on the clock. We know we could get everything done if there were no interruptions or mini-crises to slow us down. When our children are relatively co-operative, quiet and calm, they do not distract us. So we keep focusing on our tasks.

But why are we rushing and stressing? Who told us we need to lead our lives like this?

What would happen if we changed our job description to one that was less stressful? How about a job description that is about taking the time to enjoy our children and to teach them the skills, habits and values that we think they should have? Of course we still have to go to the supermarket and clean the bath and return telephone calls. But with our new job description the chores are no longer our focus. Now we are focusing on *being with the children* at the dry cleaners, *being with the children* in the car, *being with the children* while we do the washing up. After all, why did we have children? So we could focus on housework and errands? Presumably we had children so that we could be with them and enjoy them. With our new job description we now have time to enjoy our children as we teach them the right way to behave. We have time to observe, notice, think, and plan. It becomes so much easier to notice all their faltering little steps in the right direction and to Descriptively Praise them.

Can you imagine allowing yourself this new job description? There are lots of advantages:

- You will enjoy your children more and you will like them better.
- You will experience less stress and less fatigue.
- Your children will like you better.
- Your children will soon be much more pleasant, co-operative, confident and happier.
- Within weeks you will have more peace and quiet because your children will not "need" to misbehave to get your attention.
- Soon your children will be more motivated to be helpful and they will also be more skilled, so you will be doing less for them and you will have more time to call your own. Of course, we all know that it is far quicker and easier to make the bed ourselves or put the laundry away ourselves than to teach and supervise as the child learns, bit by bit, day by day, to do it properly. But persevere. Teaching and training are investments that pay dividends much sooner than parents can imagine.
- You will experience the satisfaction and confidence that comes from knowing that your children are actively learning the skills, habits and values that are important to you.

When your focus is on *being with your children* as you take care of the day-to-day chores, your children will not be a distraction or an interruption. You will have plenty of time and head space to notice and mention their many tiny steps in the right direction. Even a very annoying child does many O.K. things every day. Through practice, you will get better and better at Descriptive Praise, and pretty soon it will become second nature.

Descriptive Praise gives children what they crave and need, something that is easily as important as food, namely appreciation and approval. Children need to see that we like them as well as love them. Just as we know that for optimal physical growth children's bodies need food every day, let us also remember that for optimal emotional growth children's spirits need lots of appreciation and approval every day. The more that children hear our approval, the more eager they become to try and please us even more.

Target your child's annoying habits by noticing and mentioning every tiny moment when he is not doing that habit. In the past we had sharp attention to detail for what the child did wrong. Now I am asking you to notice not just your child's major accomplishments, but also his little efforts, even when the result is not yet satisfactory. At first you may need a metaphorical magnifying glass to help you to slow down and focus on the many times during the day when your child is not irritating you.

If you have not yet tried using Descriptive Praise, you probably cannot imagine the strength of the positive impact it can have on your children's mood and self-esteem, as well as on their behaviour, even the behaviour of difficult-to-raise or slow-to-warm-up children. For a four-week period, challenge yourself to Descriptively Praise each member of your immediate family (and that includes your partner and yourself) ten times every day. Think of Descriptive Praise as a new language. We know that the only way to learn a new language is by practising speaking the language, even though we feel foolish and awkward at first. After some time it becomes automatic and eventually you can even think in the new language.

To make this project less daunting, I have included many real-life examples of the kinds of behaviours you might Descriptively Praise and also what words you could use. The key is to identify a child's irritating behaviour (this part is usually not difficult!) and then to frequently *notice and mention* the specifics of every tiny step in the *right* direction. We will even need to notice a five-minute time span during which the child did not whinge or swear or annoy his brother.

You will notice that the children being Descriptively Praised in these examples have not done anything amazingly wonderful. That is because most children do not do amazingly wonderful things every day. But children do lots of O.K. things every day. And by noticing and mentioning the O.K. or almost-O.K. behaviour, those actions which we would normally take for granted, we will teach the child how to please us. As you get the hang of this new skill, you will be able to see how you can adapt the Descriptive Praises to your own unique scenarios. You will also probably find that you want to show your appreciation more and more and more, both because it improves behaviour so rapidly and dramatically, and also because it feels so much nicer to appreciate than to criticise.

I will give examples of how we can use Descriptive Praise to foster co-operation during the most trying times in a typical day with children, the "family flashpoints", when everyone has a short fuse. For most families, the typical flashpoints are:

A   Time pressure, especially getting ready in the mornings
B   Mealtimes, table manners and nutrition
C   Screen time (television, computers, video games, Gameboy™, etc.)
D   Keeping belongings tidy and helping with household tasks
E   Homework and home learning (including reading, revision and projects)
F   Playing independently
G   Bedtimes and sleep
H   Getting along with siblings.

Descriptive Praise for prevention and early intervention

When our children are being relatively co-operative, calm and self-reliant, we tend to use the time it frees up to get tasks done. This is completely understandable, but unfortunately it is short-sighted. Instead of taking the relative harmony for granted, we need to build on the good behaviour so that it will last as long as possible. Prevention is all about what parents can do *before* misbehaviour occurs to keep children calm and co-operative most of the time. Descriptive Praise is a very useful method of prolonging these 'good' moments. The more we Descriptively Praise, the fewer meltdowns, tantrums, confrontations and crises we will have to deal with.

Let us imagine, for example, that the children are playing contentedly by themselves or eating what has been put in front of them without a fuss or doing their homework without complaining.

If we remember to praise at all, typically we might say, "You children are playing so nicely together" or "What a good eater you are" or "You're so clever". This evaluative praise is of course better than ignoring our children and saying nothing, but it is not very effective at influencing behaviour. This is partly because it is too vague, and therefore not very believable. Also, it does not contain much information that the child can use when he wants to get more praise by behaving in a similar way again.

Descriptive Praise is valuable because it is believable. You do not make over-the-top statements that can easily be disputed. Instead you describe, very specifically and in detail, what the child is doing right or what he is not doing wrong.

To the children who are playing well together you might say, "You're sharing the Lego™ and there's no grabbing" or "I don't hear any teasing" or "For ten whole minutes you two have been sitting there drawing quietly, and neither of you has come to me with any complaints about the other one".

You can adapt the following examples to target the behaviour and motivation issues in your family. With Descriptive Praise you can capture and build on the previously invisible bits of just-O.K. behaviour for each of the family flashpoints.

As the majority of children who are smacked are under eleven, the examples are targeted to this younger age group.

A Getting ready in the mornings

1 You asked a question, and then you answered it yourself. You used your own brain.

2 You're not playing now because you know it's time to get dressed. You remembered that getting dressed comes before playing, so I didn't have to remind you.

3 I'm glad that you picked your books off the floor, without my having to say a word about it. I've noticed that you've been remembering to put things back in the right place. That shows self-reliance.

4 Just now, when your sister spilt her drink, you didn't make fun of her. You didn't even make a silly face. You're being tolerant. Thank you.

5 Thanks for not throwing your clothes around, even though you don't want to get dressed. This way the room stays tidy.

B Mealtimes, table manners and nutrition

1 Thank you for staying at the table, even though you're not hungry. That shows me you're paying attention to the rule about staying at the table until we say you can get down.

2 Even though you both want to talk, you're not interrupting each other. You're being patient.

3 I can see you're remembering to use your napkin. Your face looks nice and clean. I can hardly tell you've been eating.

4 I'm glad you tried some of the soup, even though I know you're disappointed that we're not having pizza tonight. You really wanted pizza, but you were polite and you tasted the soup.

5 Thank you for not complaining about the food. You're just eating what you want and leaving what you don't want, without even talking about it. That takes self-control.

6 What a nice, quiet, peaceful table this is. No one is arguing.

C Screen time

1 Thanks for turning it off the first time I asked, without much arguing. That's real co-operation.

2 I like how responsible you're being. You've already fed the dog and finished your homework. So now you've earned your hour of TV for tonight.

3 I noticed that you didn't shout at your sister when she wanted to watch a different programme. It's very annoying when she cries and cries, but you didn't make it worse by shouting. You just answered her in a calm, sensible voice. Too bad she doesn't always listen.

D Keeping belongings tidy and helping with household tasks

1 I'm glad to see that you brought down some cups from your room when I asked you to. And you didn't put the cups on the kitchen table. You put them in the sink. That's attention to detail. And it's less work for me.

2 I'm very pleased to see that you're putting those toys away, with no complaining, even though the baby took out some of them. You're setting her a good example.

3 I'm very glad that you're not shouting at me, even though I'm asking you to do a job you really don't want to do. I know it's not much fun for you to clean up. It's much more fun to play, isn't it? But you're controlling yourself. You're not shouting.

4 Thanks for helping your brother set the table. You shared the job. And when he put the forks on the wrong side you corrected him without making him feel bad. That was kind.

5 I noticed that after you fed Spot you didn't just leave the spoon in the sink. You washed it off very carefully. You took care of the whole job yourself, from beginning to end, and I didn't have to do any of your job. That's what I call self-reliance.

6 You remembered to put the toilet seat down. That was considerate.

E Homework and home learning (includes reading, revision and projects)

1 I can see that you remembered to write your homework in your homework diary today. That shows good sense. Now you know exactly what you have to do.

2 You have six sentences in your story, and you remembered to start five of them with a capital letter. That's attention to detail.

3 Even though you're fed up, you're not complaining or arguing. You're trying to work out the answer.

4 You answered all the questions in this exercise, even though you weren't sure of some of the answers. You didn't leave any blanks. You had a go and wrote something down for every single question. You challenged yourself.

5 I noticed just now, when you were reading out loud, that when you made a mistake, you went back and corrected it, without anyone having to tell you. It takes maturity to notice your own mistakes and then to correct them.

F Playing independently

1 You're playing by yourself so patiently and not interrupting me. I can really concentrate on what I am doing.

2 I can see you're having fun making lots of little people out of those pipe cleaners. In a little while, when I'm ready, will you show them all to me?

3 I know you were disappointed that you couldn't have a friend over. But now you're having a good time drawing. That shows flexibility.

4 You've been looking at books for ten minutes. That's a long time!

G Bedtimes and sleep

1 You got into your pyjamas, even though you wish you could stay up later for that television programme. You did what you were told.

2 You only got out of bed twice last night. And each time I took you back to bed you didn't say you were hungry. You were honest.

3 You stayed in your bed last night.

4 Your sheets are dry! You didn't wet the bed in the night.

H Getting along with siblings

1 It can't be easy having to share a room with such a messy little brother. But you're being patient with him. You're not getting cross because you know he's too little to understand.

2 It's nice to see that the two of you aren't hitting each other, even though I can see that you're both *very* angry. You each think you're right and the other one is wrong. And you didn't come to me.

3 In the past hour, you haven't said anything horrible to your brothers, even though they can be a nuisance. You've been keeping calm. You deserve to be very proud of yourself. Keeping calm isn't easy!

4 Just now your sister snatched your train, and I could see that made you angry. But you didn't hit her! You just told her in a very strong voice that you were playing with it. And you even said "thank you" when she finally let go. Very sensible behaviour! That way you didn't get into trouble.

5 You each wanted to play a different game, but you didn't argue for long. You came up with a solution all by yourselves. And neither of you came to me for help. That shows self-reliance.

6 You started out with three cars and your sister had only one, so you let her play with one of yours. You didn't have to do that, but you chose to do it, all by yourself. That was very mature.

To make your Descriptive Praise even more meaningful, you can summarise what you have noticed by mentioning a quality, as I have shown in some of the examples. Here is a list of the top ten qualities that parents say they want their children to develop:

1 Co-operation
2 Friendly, sensible tone of voice
3 Sharing
4 Patience
5 Consideration
6 Self-reliance and common sense
7 Self-control
8 Honesty
9 Courage
10 Paying attention to details

The more often we mention, as part of our Descriptive Praises, that the child has shown these positive qualities, the sooner the child will be able to "re-invent" himself.

Sometimes we need to be reminded about our child's positive attributes and qualities. This is especially true of the child whose sensitive, intense or impulsive temperament can drive us crazy.

Familiarise yourself with this A-Z list of positive qualities so that you will more readily notice them in your child. The more you look for the good qualities in your child, the more of them you will find. Soon you will be adding new words to this list.

accepting	efficient	kind	resourceful
adventurous	empathy	knowledgeable	responsibility
affectionate	encouraging	lateral thinking	safety-conscious
alert	entertaining	leader	self-control
amusing	enthusiastic	loving	self-reliance
animated	fast-thinking	loyal	sensible
appreciative	first time	making an effort	serious
articulate	flexible	manners	sharing
artistic	focus	mature	studious
attentive to detail	following	motivated	sympathetic
brave	instructions	neat	thorough
calm	forgiving	noticing	thoughtful
capable	friendly	observant	thrifty
careful	generous	optimistic	time-keeping
caring	gentle	orderly	tolerance
cautious	giving	organised	trusting
challenging	good example	patient	trustworthy
oneself	good-natured	paying attention	truthful
common sense	good sport	peace-maker	unafraid
concentrating	grateful	perseverance	unashamed
confident	grown-up	persistent	understanding
conscientious	healthy	playful	unusual solution
considerate	helpful	positive	useful
consistent	honest	practical	versatile
co-operative	humour	prepared	warm
courageous	imaginative	problem-solver	welcoming
cuddly	independent	prompt	willing
curious	industrious	questioning	wise
determined	initiative	quiet	witty
eager	interesting	ready	
early-riser	inventive	relaxed	
easy-going	keep promises	reliable	

Physical immaturity

There is another aspect of living with children that parents can use Descriptive Praise to improve. I have already mentioned that many children with difficult-to-raise or slow-to-warm-up temperaments are often physically immature in certain areas, even though they may be very bright in other ways. The physical immaturity most commonly takes the form of weak fine-motor skills, including poor eye-hand co-ordination.

The child who finds certain tasks difficult soon learns to avoid both his own frustration and his parents' annoyance by opting out of those activities as much as he can manage to get away with. Because he does not practise, he does not improve. Immature fine-motor skills can lead to problems as diverse as an unwillingness to dress himself; messy eating; always wanting to play active, noisy games or to be entertained (because the usual age-appropriate "quiet" activities, such as drawing, puzzles or Lego™, are just too difficult and frustrating to be rewarding), difficulty throwing or catching a ball; being too rough so breaking things unintentionally, and of course, messy handwriting.

Subtle specific learning difficulties such as the above are not easy to spot. Much of it looks like carelessness, laziness, selfishness or even rudeness. And after a while the child who is continually told off for being a way that he cannot help being is very likely to become careless or rude. We need to remember that his unacceptable behaviour is born out of a genuine difficulty which has gone unrecognised and was therefore unintentionally mishandled by parents and teachers.

There are techniques available that can help this child to start wanting, and therefore to start trying, to improve. Only by harnessing his long-dormant motivation will we see any significant improvements. Descriptive Praise is one of those techniques. It is powerful enough to re-awaken in this child the desire to please his parents and teachers and the desire to be his best self:

- "You've done up five buttons on your shirt. I know it took you time but you did it."
- "You're being so careful, carrying the plate with both hands."
- "You didn't spill any of the soup on the table and there's none on your shirt."
- "You didn't give up, and you finished the whole page."

Points to remember

1 As well as Descriptively Praising what your child does right, we also need to Descriptively Praise the absence of the wrong (or annoying)

behaviour. Even when a child is not doing much right at the moment, we can foster goodwill and increase motivation by talking about what he is not doing wrong:

- "You're not grabbing. You're just looking with your eyes."
- "Thanks for not interrupting."
- "It's so quiet in the back seat."
- "You finished all your sums, without any complaining."

2 Most misbehaviour is minor rather than major. It is impulsive and thoughtless, and often it is over as quickly as it started, for example, grabbing, interrupting, stepping on a book instead of stepping over it, saying "Why?" in response to an instruction. So a useful strategy, when your child does something annoying, is to wait a few seconds. As soon as the child stops that behaviour, or even pauses for breath, *jump in with Descriptive Praise*! For example:

- "You stopped arguing, even though you're not happy about what I said."
- "Now you're not talking with your mouth full."
- "You're not grabbing now. You're being polite."
- "I'm so glad you stopped banging the chair. It's much more peaceful now."
- "No one's shouting."

3 As you have seen, most of what you will be Descriptively Praising will be actions that do not *yet* come easily or naturally to your child. The Descriptive Praise is what will motivate him to keep trying and therefore to keep improving. At first you will Descriptively Praise every time you notice the good behaviour, or even a rough approximation of it. After you see that a child is regularly doing a certain thing right, e.g. flushing the loo without being told, saying Hello to a neighbour, saying please and thank you, putting his cup in the sink, not grabbing the biggest piece of cake, etc., you can drop back to praising that behaviour once a day, then every few days. For example:

- "I haven't seen you chewing with your mouth open for three whole days."
- "I didn't hear you say you were bored all weekend. Even though you couldn't watch TV, you thought of other things to do."

4 When we are feeling very pleased and loving, we may be tempted to say, "You're such an honest boy," or "You're so brave". I always warn parents against making blanket statements like these because the child can vividly remember many times when he was *not* honest, brave,

tolerant, helpful, etc., so he does not believe the statement. He may feel guilty or anxious that he has managed to fool his parents into believing that he is a better person than he knows himself to be. He may even lose respect for parents who seem so gullible. Or he may assume that we are lying to him. Instead, we need to link the quality to a specific action:

- "Today you were careful not to drop the ornaments."
- "Right now you are staying calm and not whingeing, even though this is frustrating."
- "That was a helpful thing you did, opening the door for me."
- "I saw you being gentle with the kitten. You didn't squeeze her."
- "Not even one bit of Lego™ left on the floor! That's what I call attention to detail."

5 Do not spoil the positive impact of your Descriptive Praise by adding a veiled criticism:

- "For once, you didn't argue."
- "Why can't you be like this all the time?"
- "You see how nice things are when you behave."
- "Finally!"

6 When you want to give your child an instruction, find something to Descriptively Praise first. This will get his attention and increase his willingness.

7 Do not be afraid to repeat the same Descriptive Praise every few minutes, using slightly different words. For example, if you are in church, temple or synagogue, you could say with a big smile each time: "You're being very quiet." "You're so quiet." "You're not talking." "Thank you for being so quiet." "You're sitting so quietly". "You're waiting so patiently." "You're not saying anything". Parents who have done this regularly report that within a few weeks the child becomes very proud of himself and is keen to maintain his new reputation.

Descriptive Praise for crisis management

Even when the child is defiantly unco-operative he will be influenced in a positive direction by our appreciation and approval. It is important to combine our Descriptive Praises with an acknowledgement of how angry or upset he may be feeling:

- "Even though you don't want to share, you're not grabbing the toy away from the baby."

- "I can see you're very angry with me. But you're not screaming (or hitting or swearing or storming out – whatever your child might, in his anger, be tempted to do). You're controlling yourself. I'm proud of you."

Sentence starters

You will have noticed that most of the Descriptive Praise sample sentences start with the word "you". As you become more comfortable with "catching them being good," you will start to experiment with injecting more variety into how you start your Descriptive Praises. One way to do this is to show how their O.K. behaviour makes you feel. In addition to smiling and looking pleased, you can say:

- "I'm pleased to see that...."
- "I've noticed that you remembered to...."
- "Three nights in a row now...."
- "Today, you didn't once...."
- "I can hear...."
- "In the past week...."
- "I remember that...."
- "In the past you....., but now you...."
- "I'm so happy that...."
- "I love it when you...."
- "I feel good when I see...."
- "It gives me so much pleasure when...."
- "I like it when...."
- "I really appreciate that you aren't...."
- "Thank you for not...."
- "You're still...."
- "Yesterday...."
- "It always impresses me when...."
- "Even though I could see you didn't want to, you...."
- "Nowadays you usually...."
- "I see that you...."

Chapter 11

Frequently asked questions about Descriptive Praise

A   How can we find actions to Descriptively Praise when the child is not doing anything good?

> *"How can I get myself to Descriptively Praise ten times a day when I am so annoyed at my child for the constant stream of irritating behaviour all day long? I feel guilty admitting this, but many days I don't feel like praising him even once!"*

There are times, for all parents, when you find yourself feeling very negative about your child. At these times it will seem as if there is very, very little to appreciate. But a child will not change until we change. And the most effective strategy I know for helping children to change requires us to start noticing and mentioning their positive actions and good qualities and to *keep it up*. Here is a tried and tested way to come up with Descriptive Praises when you just cannot seem to think of any. Buy yourself some time and sanity by locking yourself in the bathroom with a pad and pencil. Take a few quiet minutes to jot down a list of this child's four or five most irritating habits. Now make sure you notice and mention *whenever* he is not doing those annoying behaviours. Most children, *even* the sensitive, intense, impulsive, over-active ones who can so easily annoy us, are doing lots of O.K. things every day. And even more importantly, at any given moment there are lots of wrong things they are *not* doing. Descriptive Praise helps children to *feel like* co-operating.

Even when your child is deliberately provoking you (whether subtly or blatantly), keep Descriptively Praising. Of course, this is not what you feel like doing. Every fibre of your being is screaming at you to tell him off or smack him or give him "a taste of his own medicine". But since, in the past, that has not brought you the result you want, try this new technique. Descriptive Praise has a much better track record than criticism for motivating children to show us their best side.

If you really cannot find anything to Descriptively Praise, you may be expecting too much too soon. We need to have realistic expectations. That does *not* mean lowering our standards. It means that we need to start from whatever level the child is currently at and notice all the tiny steps in the right direction.

If you have established clear rules, it becomes much easier to find things to Descriptively Praise. Even when your child is doing something wrong, think of a rule that he is *not* breaking at that moment.

Particularly with children who are frequently defiant or very impulsive and immature, you will have much more to Descriptively Praise if you are willing to spend a few minutes, five or ten times a day, preparing for success by doing what I call "talk-throughs". A talk-through is a very useful technique which maximises the likelihood of your child co-operating by jogging his memory about your expectations and rules. Unfortunately, when we are reminding our children about what to do and how to do it, often they are not really listening, especially if our tone of voice is even slightly annoyed or impatient. A talk-through is different in four important respects:

1 The talk-through happens before the event, before the child has had the opportunity to misbehave.

2 In a talk-through, it is the *child*, not the adult, who does the telling. The child says what he should do and how he should do it, with the parent merely asking leading questions to make sure that all important aspects of the desired behaviour are covered.

3 The child is required to say *in detail* what he should do and not do. That way it will stick in his mind better.

4 The only time that the parent will switch from asking to telling is when the child says something that is not accurate. Once you have clarified that rule or routine, ask the question again several more times, to help the child remember it and take it seriously.

Here is an example told to me by a mother. One of the flashpoints she was having great difficulty with was table manners. In order to keep her impulsive child's attention from wandering, during each talk-through the mother addressed only the most annoying behaviour, rather than everything she wanted to improve.

First she sat down on the floor next to him where he was playing and chatted briefly about what he was making. Then she said:

Parent (P)   *"It's almost dinner time. Tell me what you have to do at dinner."*
Child (C)   *"I have to be good."*
P   *"I'm glad you know you have to be good. What will you do when you're being good?"*

C	(Long pause) *"I have to stay in my chair and not say 'Yuk'."*
P	*"You remembered two of our rules. You're going to stay sitting down for the whole meal until what?"*
C	*"Till I've finished."*
P	*"No. You have to stay in your chair even after you're finished eating. You have to stay until Daddy or I say what?"*
C	*"Till you say I can get down."*
P	*"That's the rule. Now tell me again. You'll only get down when?"*
C	*"When you say I can get down."*
P	*"I can see you know that rule. And why aren't you going to say 'Yuk'?"*
C	*"Because ... it hurts your feelings?"*
P	*"That's right. You don't want to hurt my feelings. What will you do if you have some food on your plate that you don't like, instead of saying 'Yuk'?"*
C	*"I won't say 'Yuk'."*
P	*"I'm happy about that. What will you do instead?"*
C	*"I'll just leave it and I won't say anything horrible."*
P	*"That's what grown-ups do. You're getting more grown-up every day."*

The above talk-through, which lasted only a few minutes, resulted in much better (although not perfect) behaviour. At dinner, the mother then made a point of Descriptively Praising her child for following the two rules which they had just talked through. She also Descriptively Praised a lot of other good behaviours that had not even been mentioned in the talk-through: saying the occasional "please", not wiping his hands on his shirt, not interrupting, keeping his legs down, not grabbing, sitting up straight. The mother reported that in subsequent talk-throughs her child mentioned as rules the behaviours that the mother had made a point of consistently Descriptively Praising. That is an example of how Descriptive Praise teaches children the appropriate ways to behave; we do not need to lecture or criticise.

B   How can we help ourselves remember to Descriptively Praise?

"This is all so new to me, this idea of praising all the time. How do I keep myself from getting distracted and just forgetting to do it?"

I have suggested that you start by Descriptively Praising each child ?
partner and yourself ten times a day. If you do it religiously, you w'
in a week or two it becomes much easier to remember to notice

the O.K. behaviours. In fact, you will become keen to Descriptively Praise each one even *more than ten times a day*. There are two reasons that it becomes easier and easier to remember to Descriptively Praise. One reason is that we are establishing a new habit. The other reason is that there will be an increase in O.K. behaviour because Descriptive Praise shows children (and partners!) how to get our positive attention, which is what they want and need.

At first, before your ten-a-day habit is solidly established, you may find that you forget to say your ten Descriptive Praises. Here are some solutions that parents in our "Calmer, Easier, Happier Parenting" seminars have come up with to solve the problem of forgetting:

- When you are kissing your children goodnight, say all the Descriptive Praises that eluded you during the busy day.
- Use mealtimes, when you have a captive audience, to catch up on Descriptive Praises.
- When the other parent comes home or a family friend drops by or you bump into an acquaintance on the way to the shops – Descriptively Praise your child to the adult in the child's presence. He will be listening and absorbing, even if he seems oblivious.
- Establish some new habits for yourself. For example, say a Descriptive Praise each time you:
  - get in the car
  - drop your child off or collect him from school
  - supervise bath time, brushing teeth and getting dressed
  - see your child doing homework.
- For teenagers, whom you may rarely see on some days, write a daily list and put it on their pillow. Many parents of surly adolescents have reported success using these lists of Descriptive Praises. Parents have been touched to see that their ultra-cool teens, who never mentioned the existence of the lists, soon started smiling more, swearing and slamming doors less, spending more time with the family, doing what they were asked with less of an argument. A number of parents told us that months and even years later, while cleaning out their teenagers' rooms, they found bundles of carefully-preserved Descriptive Praise lists. There is no question that Descriptive Praise makes a powerful, positive impact on behaviour, confidence, motivation and self-esteem. It is too powerful a tool not to use daily, indeed many times daily.

C Why do we sometimes resist Descriptively Praising our children, and how can we motivate ourselves to Descriptively Praise even when we don't feel like doing it?

"All my generation were told off when we did something stupid or downright bad, and it didn't do us any harm. We grew up to be responsible and hard-working and reliable, which is more than I can say for the younger generation. Why do we have to pussyfoot around our children? Why can't they take constructive criticism and learn from it, as we did?"

"My daughter is quite bright. Surely she'll be able to see through all this and realise that I'm just using a psychological technique on her?"

"I'm too tired and annoyed to be so patient. Even though I know I shouldn't, it's much easier to shout and moan at them. How do I stay calm and positive?"

"It doesn't seem morally right to have to fake being pleased when really I'm fed up with her and not feeling truly appreciative. Isn't being honest about my feelings more important?"

At first you might feel ill at ease and unconfident when you first commit yourself to such an intense degree of positivity. Stick with it. It gets easier and more comfortable. And you will get hooked on the results: a calmer, easier, happier family.

In case you're thinking that all this Descriptive Praise is highly artificial, you're right! Nagging children and telling them off seem to be far more "natural" or at least habitual reactions, but unfortunately they are also counter-productive. Criticism does not help children to improve their behaviour. And in the case of the difficult-to-raise children and the slow-to-warm-up children, over the years our very natural tendency to criticise often makes their behaviour worse. So I am suggesting that we practise a new way of talking, Descriptive Praise, that does not come naturally at first. Force yourself to Descriptively Praise, even when you are so annoyed that you do not feel or sound sincere. Even insincere Descriptive Praise is much more effective at improving behaviour than sincere criticism and shouting. Eventually the Descriptive Praise will become second nature and you will find that you are feeling sincere when you say it. The effort we will need to expend to establish this new habit within ourselves is an investment that will quickly pay us huge dividends.

When you do not feel the slightest bit appreciative, it is hard to remember that going through the motions of Descriptively Praising will actually make you feel better. It helps to understand that we do not need to feel calm or positive. All we need to do is *temporarily act calmer*. This "act" helps children calm down and start co-operating faster than our display of anger would. A delightful bonus of acting calm is that it often leads, sooner than one might imagine, to feeling calm.

To a parent it may not seem like praise unless you say "Good" or some other evaluative word, such as "Brilliant! Terrific! Wonderful!" The parent may not understand how the child will know that Descriptive Praise is really praise, if it is simply a description, with no evaluative word stuck in. At first, you will probably add an evaluative comment, out of habit. It is not a sin or crime to say "Good" or "Super" or "Wonderful". However, most of the small steps in the right direction that you will be Descriptively Praising are not super, wonderful, marvellous or brilliant. I suggest it is more effective to smile a lot, use a very pleased tone of voice, elaborate on your Descriptive Praise and give a big hug.

At first your child may well think you've taken leave of your senses. But that is not a good enough reason not to do it. If something is right (in this case, both respectful and effective), it is right, even if it mystifies our children at first. I suggest that all the adults who live at home sit down with your children and explain to them the following:

a   In the past, you made many mistakes as parents (this will get their attention, though they may be disconcertingly ready to agree with you).
b   You used ineffective strategies to try to get your children to co-operate and improve, such as nagging, shouting or smacking.
c   You've now learned about a more effective strategy, Descriptive Praise.
d   You will be practising this new strategy from now on.
e   You can't guarantee that you'll be perfect. There will be times when you will forget or when you won't do a good job with the new strategy. But you know that with repeated practice, you'll improve.

Your children may be convinced that you will not be able to keep it up. For your sake and theirs, prove them wrong.

D Why might a child resist Descriptive Praise, and what can we do about it?

"I tried Descriptive Praise a few times as soon as I learned about it. But it backfired on me. He seems to hate being praised! He even stuck his fingers in his ears and started humming loudly to drown me out. I didn't want to upset him, so I stopped doing it. Why didn't it work?"

"My little one sometimes does the opposite of what I've just praised her for. It seems to remind her of the bad behaviour. Surely that's the opposite of what we're trying to achieve. Shouldn't I just let sleeping dogs lie and say nothing when she's being good?"

"My teenager says I'm being patronising. How can I learn to say it in a way that he'll accept?"

Do not expect your child to transform magically overnight. In fact, at first he may even argue with you about the Descriptive Praise or become visibly upset or try to tune you out. This phase does not last long and is far more common amongst difficult-to-raise and slow-to-warm-up children. Here are some possible reasons for the occasional negative reaction and what parents can do to move through this phrase as quickly as possible. A number of these scenarios may apply to your child:

1 It feels like an insult to children if we Descriptively Praise "small steps in the right direction" for behaviours they have already mastered. To avoid this, we can Descriptively Praise the fact that the behaviour is becoming a habit. For example, instead of saying, "Thanks for flushing the loo" to a child who usually remembers to, we can say, "Most of the time you remember to flush the loo and wash your hands, and you don't leave the towel on the floor any more."

2 Your child may be embarrassed to admit to himself that certain mature behaviour still needs to be reinforced by Descriptive Praise. He would like to believe that he has long since mastered certain behaviours, such as:
   - turning lights off when leaving a room
   - not drumming on the table
   - speaking quietly indoors
   - looking at the person who is talking
   - starting homework or household tasks without having to be reminded.

3 Particularly with teenagers, cultivate a conversational tone, rather than an exclamatory tone. Smile and make eye-contact to show that you are very pleased. It will be much less embarrassing for him if you keep your tone low-key. There is another reason for this advice. I am suggesting that you start with ten Descriptive Praises per day per family member and gradually work your way up to scores of Descriptive Praises every day. If you were to turn each of these Descriptive Praises into a big, excited exclamation, you would wear yourself out emotionally.

4 Boys are often labelled naughty, rebellious and oppositional. They are criticised more than girls are, both at home and at school. This often leads to negative attention-seeking and to the gradual development of a self-image of being bad, unlikable or "thick". Because of this entrenched low self-esteem, it may take longer with boys for the Descriptive Praise to start working.

5 Your child may have been in the habit of getting negative attention for negative behaviour for years. Positive attention can be unsettling at first. A child who has been told off a lot may not believe, at first, that you could possibly be that pleased with him that many times each day. Your child might be so uncomfortable with his new persona that he even asks you to stop praising him. Don't stop praising him! Descriptive Praise is like medicine: it works even if we don't like the taste. It may even take a few months before he feels comfortable with getting positive attention for positive behaviour.

6 An intense or angry child almost seems to enjoy the excitement of seeing you get upset. It is not so interesting when you stay calm and positive. He may be hooked on the power to wind you up, a skill he has perfected to a fine art. When you keep mentioning the positive, the child can see that you are in charge of your emotions. This can make him angry. He may have come to associate parental love with the intense emotions that accompany shouting, arguing, telling off and smacking. So when you stay calm and positive it may seem to the child as if you do not care about him any more. A child who is not very good at things (e.g. school, sports, making friends) may come to feel that the only thing he is "good at" is making adults angry. When this child starts hearing a lot of Descriptive Praise, he may start panicking inwardly, worrying that he is losing his grip in the one area where he felt successful and powerful. His self-image as someone who gets into trouble a lot is being shaken up. A child who has carved out a niche

for himself by being "bad" may worry that there will be nothing much very special about him if he becomes "good", and that no one will notice him. His familiar self-image may not give up without a fight. So persevere!

7 In the first few weeks, an impulsive child may react to Descriptive Praise by occasionally doing the exact opposite of what you just praised him for. That is because the Descriptive Praise reminds him of the misbehaviour and then his impulsivity gets the better of him. This is very annoying, of course, and it feels as if you are going backwards, so you may be tempted to give up on the Descriptive Praise. Keep Descriptively Praising even if the behaviour gets worse temporarily before it gets better. If you persevere, this phase will not last long. Soon he will naturally and automatically begin to try to control himself.

8 The sensitive child's negative emotions may be re-activated. At first, the Descriptive Praise may, paradoxically, remind him of all the times when he has been criticised for doing that thing wrong. A child who has been told off a lot and then starts being Descriptively Praised may assume that his parents expect him to behave this well all the time. He knows that he can't so he does not even want to start and then feels like a failure when he can't keep it up.

9 For maximum positive effect, turn your Descriptive Praise sentences into paragraphs. The child who does not really believe that he is capable of pleasing his parents is the child who has been "verbally smacked" far more than is good for him. In self-defence, he may have shut down, becoming "parent-deaf". His defences may be so strong that he barely hears or registers short Descriptive Praises such as, "Thanks for putting your plate in the sink". But when we take the time and make the effort to turn these one-liners into paragraphs, this child is far more likely to hear us. You might say, "Thanks for putting your plate in the sink. I didn't even have to tell you. You remembered without my having to say a word. That shows a mature sense of responsibility. You're not expecting people to do things for you when you can do them yourself. Thanks". At this point your child will probably look around to see what else he can put in the sink!

Chapter 12
General principles for managing Start and Stop behaviours

Descriptive Praise and Preparing For Success talk-throughs are very effective for the prevention of much misbehaviour and for early intervention when things start to go wrong. But even with consistent use of these skills, it is completely normal that a small amount of misbehaviour will not be nipped in the bud. Depending on how it is handled, the misbehaviour that remains can *be defused or it can escalate*. In the next three chapters I will discuss how to handle the most common types of misbehaviour, those which are deliberate as well as those which are the product of immaturity, impulsivity, habit and attention-seeking.

A very small amount of misbehaviour is a deliberate attempt to upset the parent. When the child no longer feels that his parents like or approve of him, he may become so angry and bitter, so desperate and unhappy, that he misbehaves on purpose, driven by feelings of fury and revenge. Family relationships *can* be mended, even when they have deteriorated to this extent. With the Calmer, Easier, Happier Parenting skills it is possible to restore goodwill all round.

Children who are sensitive, intense and impulsive are easily upset. In particular, they are quickly angered by an adult saying "No" or "Stop" or "Don't". This is partly because they have heard these words so many times. They feel as if they are constantly being criticised, blamed and forced to do things they hate. And due to their impulsivity and intensity, it is hard for them to let go of wanting what they want.

To avoid full-scale tantrums and to maximise the likelihood of compliance, we need to think carefully before we speak and act. The following strategies can calm down a potentially explosive situation and help children to want to co-operate.

This chapter talks about the strategies that are useful for achieving co-operation with both Stop behaviours and Start behaviours.

1 Consistency

All the adults in the home need to agree on the rules. What often happens is that the mother, who is with the children a lot, makes the rules, or metes out the consequences, in the father's absence. When he comes home he feels somewhat confused about the routines, like an outsider. So he may hesitate to discipline, preferring to leave most of it to the mother. Also he may be reluctant to be the "bad guy" during his few precious hours with his children. The mother, in turn, may feel angry when the father does not back her up. Children are quick to divide and conquer, taking advantage of confusion, guilt and resentment.

It is not always easy for parents to agree. And unfortunately, "agreeing to disagree" is not a workable option because children react badly to lack of consistency. One of the reasons that a united front can be difficult to achieve is that each parent may have a very different temperament. There is a saying, "Opposites attract". In reality, "At first, opposites attract. Then they annoy". Sparks will fly between an easy-going parent and a more anxious one or between a parent who values responsibility highly and one who puts more emphasis on self-expression.

Usually parents are willing to work at setting aside their differences and aligning their values as soon as they realise how important consistency is for their children's well-being. Even when parents disagree on many things, they *do* generally agree that the welfare of their children comes first.

The most basic aspect of a United Front is not arguing in front of the children. It takes two to have an argument, so each parent needs to be responsible for not responding negatively if the other parent starts to argue. This becomes much easier to do if parents are willing to regularly sit down and talk through which rules and routines, and which rewards and consequences, they want to see implemented. When parents need to learn to pull together as a team, this is what I suggest:

Set aside fifteen minutes a day for what I call "solution talk". This can be done over the telephone. Choose *one* area of confusion or conflict within the family, and both contribute ideas for possible solutions. It is important to spend no more than *one sentence* on describing the problem and then immediately focus on possible solutions.

One family recorded this segment of one of their solutions-talk:

Mother (M):*Let's talk about breakfast.*
Father (F): *What's the problem? Don't make a problem when there isn't one.*
M: *There is. There is a problem. For me, because I'm here. They're too busy watching cartoons to eat properly. Tom takes forever to finish and then he plays when he should be getting dressed. And Wendy...*

F:	*Wait. No more problems! Let's just solve what you said. We can talk about the other stuff tomorrow.*
M:	*O.K. Solutions. Umm… Really I know we should keep the TV off while they are eating.*
F:	*Why do they need to watch it at all in the morning? I would be happy if the TV didn't go on at all in the morning. Then you could actually have a conversation.*
M:	*But, but… O.K. They'll make a fuss… but I guess they'll get used to it.*
F:	*And then they can concentrate on their cereal.*
M:	*One mum at the parenting class said that now she makes her children get completely dressed before breakfast. Even put their schoolbags by the door. And hair brushed.*
F:	*That wouldn't work with Wendy. She's such a slowcoach.*
M:	*Stay positive!*
F:	*(groan) O.K. Positive. Let's try it.*
M:	*For how long? Two weeks?*
F:	*Yes. Two weeks. What if they don't finish eating and it's time to leave?*
M:	*I'll get them up ten minutes earlier.*
F:	*O.K. But let's prepare for success. We should tell them. Otherwise it's not fair.*
M:	*Let's tell them that it'll start on Wednesday. So they have two more days of morning telly. Then no more.*
F:	*And we should do some Reflective Listening if they say it's not fair. But not argue back.*
M:	*Fine. – time's up and we've managed to stay positive!*

Single parents also need support, and having frequent solution talks with a friend is an excellent way to get feedback and support. The friend need not even be a parent. A listening ear, a compassionate presence is often all that is needed to help shift the focus from complaining about problems to seeking and then implementing solutions.

A United Front means parents backing each other up. If one parent is running into problems with misbehaviour, the other parent needs to stop what he or she is doing and give strong support. Often it is enough to say, "Do what your mother (or father) says", in a very calm, serious voice. Children will not usually ignore or defy this United Front although they may still test to see what they can get away with, especially if parents have not been consistent in the past. Sometimes parents are reluctant to back each other up in this way because of the mistaken notion that the child will feel the parents are "ganging up" on him and feel intimidated. There is nothing unfair about a United Front! It sends the children a very clear signal that both parents agree about the behaviour required, and that both parents care enough to actively enforce it.

There is another, very important type of consistency that parents ignore at their peril. Each parent needs to be consistent from one day to the next and in all places. That means that a rule is a rule, regardless of whether you are in a laid-back, easy-going mood or a frazzled, wit's-end mood. It also means that you need to brave the stares of strangers in Sainsbury's and follow through with the same discipline as you would at home.

2   Clarifying the family's rules and routines

The first step, as we saw, is making sure that both of the parents know and understand and have agreed on the rules and routines. The next step is to make sure that the children know and understand them, even though they may not agree with them.

When children know exactly what they should and should not do, and where and when and how and with whom, they are far more likely to get into the habit of co-operation. Making the rules absolutely clear is not a magic wand that will turn a child into an angel, but it *will*, over time, help the child to take what you say seriously. Clear expectations go a long way towards reducing the annoying "game" of testing to see what they can get away with.

There are two stages to making our expectations clear. First we need to make sure, before the misbehaviour begins, that the child knows what he should and should not do. This is best achieved by doing many short "talk-throughs" throughout the day, whenever a potentially problematic incident or event is about to happen. As we saw in Chapter 10, the talk-through is so effective for several important reasons. It prepares for success, before anything has gone wrong. The child is still calm so he is more motivated to listen and take in what is being said. The parent is calm so she can choose her words carefully and stay positive and Descriptively Praise. In a talk-through the child's brain is making the effort to remember or figure out the right thing to do. This internal process activates the child's long-term memory and motivation far more effectively than when we are telling the child and he is nodding wisely (while he is thinking about something else).

The second stage to making sure that our children know exactly what they should and should not do is the follow-through that comes after the event, either after the misbehaviour or after the O.K. behaviour. Earlier we saw how Descriptive Praise effectively motivates children to do the right thing and also clarifies exactly what the right thing to do is. I will now discuss the follow-through for the not-O.K. behaviour.

3   Do not indulge in "armchair discipline"

Whenever you want your child to stop or start doing something, immediately stop what you are doing and go to where the child is. Proximity is very powerful; it is a form of body language that conveys purpose and seriousness. You may well find that your presence is enough to get your child back on track. Many parents report that as they are in the act of crossing the room, the child (who a moment ago seemed oblivious to everything except what he was doing) either stops the misbehaviour or modifies it considerably. When this happens, it is a perfect opportunity for the parent to Descriptively Praise: "I didn't even need to tell you to stop banging the table. You stopped all by yourself".

4   Stay friendly

Remember to smile and to speak in a low, calm voice, even if you are feeling stressed or annoyed. When we appear angry, children often react with anger or defensiveness. When we make the effort to stay calm and friendly, children are more likely to meet us half-way, gradually becoming less antagonistic and more willing to co-operate.

When we become visibly upset over misbehaviour, it sends out a message of weakness. And it also sets a poor example. We want our children to learn how to take events in their stride without getting too upset, so we need to show them how it is done. The more we practise, the easier it becomes.

5   Reduce the number of instructions you give

Do not give unnecessary instructions, and do not repeat your instructions. We want to avoid an atmosphere of constant nagging, bossing and correcting, for several reasons:

- It annoys and upsets all concerned, undermining everyone's goodwill.
- Children learn to tune us out until they detect that rising pitch of parental hysteria which warns them that they had better pay attention *now*. This results, over time, in a vicious circle. The children ignore us. We repeat, remind and nag even more. The children find this very disagreeable so pay even less attention. The converse is also true.

Parents find that the less they say, the more carefully children listen. So we have to make our words count.

- As important as immediate co-operation is to the smooth functioning of the family, there is something even more important that we want from our children. That is the habit of self-reliance and using their common sense. We want our children to tell themselves what to do. They will not form that habit if we are doing their thinking for them and telling them what to do.

Instead of repeating and reminding, arrange the physical environment so that temptations are reduced. It then becomes far easier for your child to get into the habit of usually doing the right thing, e.g.

- To prevent arguments about being warm enough, in the winter remove all summer clothes from the children's cupboard.
- At the dinner table, seat siblings at diagonal corners so that they cannot poke or kick each other.
- Pack away all but a few toys to limit the amount of mess that an impulsive child could create by dumping them all out, treading on them and then not wanting to tidy them away.
- On school mornings do not allow the television to be switched on as it distracts children from what they need to be focusing on.
- On school mornings when children want to play together or if they squabble when they should be getting ready for school, put their clothes in separate rooms, and insist that they get dressed there.

Make rules easy to remember:

- Instead of ball-throwing or furniture-climbing or bed-bouncing being permissible in certain rooms but not in others, have a rule that these activities are not allowed at all indoors. Of course, to make this stick, you will need to provide daily time, preferably out-of-doors, when children can burn off their excess energy in acceptable ways.

"Worst first"

- A very useful rule is that the television or computer *never* goes on until homework, reading and revision are completed to the parents' satisfaction. For most children, screen time is a highly motivating reward that they will work for and behave well for.
- Most children wake up hungry. You can use this fact to motivate a dawdler. Have the rule that breakfast happens only after the child is completely dressed and hair brushed.

Use visual reminders that you can point to, rather than repeating yourself. The following morning list has eased tempers and improved co-operation in many households:

- Get dressed
- Brush hair
- Make bed
- Eat breakfast
- Put bowl and cup in sink
- Clean teeth
- Play if there is time.

Similar lists can be made for homework, bath time, bedtime, and even for activities that take place away from home, e.g. car journeys, church services and parties. These lists work best when:

- Parents and children sit down together to make them.
- The children contribute their ideas first, with parents asking them leading questions to prompt children to think of the missing items.
- The lists are easy for children to read and understand
    - poster size at first
    - big print
    - legible writing but not in capital letters as they are harder to read
    - fewest words possible and lots of white space
    - use pictures for non-readers
    - laminate for away-from-home activities.
- Parents make the time to use these lists as opportunities to Descriptively Praise:
    "You've already done 1 and 2 on your list and with no reminders. What a peaceful morning so far!"
    Then point to the next task on the list *with a smile.*

Of course there will be times and circumstances when rules, routines and instructions cannot be covered by a list. You can prompt the child to remind himself:

- Stop what you are doing and make a point of waiting expectantly for 10 or 20 seconds to see if the child will notice what he has to do.
- You can "plant a seed" in his mind. That way it is *his* brain that is doing the work. For example: If it is time to leave and your child is about to dash out without his coat, you can say quite loudly "I'm putting on my coat". If that does not jog his mind, you can add "What do *you* need to do now (or next)?"

6   Only give a direct instruction when you are almost certain that the child will comply

We know what happens when we give an instruction to a child who is angry or attention-seeking or who is very involved in what he is doing. The child ignores us or defies us. Then we are tempted to repeat, remind, shout ... and smack. As a result, the child gets angrier. And then so do we. We can avoid this waste of time and goodwill. When the child is in an unco-operative or unfriendly mood, our first job is to help him shift into a more positive state of mind.

You may feel that you do not have the time to devote to helping him feel more co-operative or motivated. But think how much time is wasted if we don't take a bit of time to do this. You may also feel that the child should automatically respect you authority as the parent and just obey, without your having to spend time getting him into the right mood. Of course, life would be simpler if our children were robots! As adults, we only respect people who have *earned* our respect. And the same is true of children. We do need to earn the respect of our children.

Also, as a preventative measure, spending 15 to 30 minutes each day playing with our children helps them to become more amenable. You might be willing to make the time for this, but you may be worried because you and your child have absolutely nothing in common, so could never agree on how to spend it. In such a situation, you can sit next to him on the floor where he is playing and start chatting and interacting. As long as you resist the urge to give advice, he will be having fun, even if you aren't.

Quality time is most effective when no siblings are present. Children are at their best when they can relax, knowing that for a short time they do not need to share, or fight for, your attention. With some thought, this can often be arranged; for example, one-to-one quality time can be squeezed in while one child is at school, sleeping or playing independently.

The techniques I have already mentioned are very useful for increasing children's motivation to co-operate and for decreasing resentment and negative attention-seeking. But you will also need strategies that you can apply in the heat of the moment, when you can see that your angry child is not likely to comply.

- Children get very absorbed in whatever they are doing, and it can feel like a painful wrench to them when they have to shift gears quickly, especially if they are expected to shift from an activity they are enjoying to an activity that is not appealing. We can ease the transition by having a count-down.

"In ten minutes it will be time to put the Lego™ away."

Be willing to say this again at five minutes and at two minutes. Each time your child hears what he will soon be doing, he makes a mental picture of it. Without his even realising it, he is getting used to the impending transition. By the time you say "Time's up", your child will usually be used to the idea that he needs to do whatever you have asked. Parents are amazed and delighted to see that the child will often begin to do the right thing even before he has used up all the allotted time. Many parents do this type of counting down for Start behaviours, such as turning off the computer to have a bath. But it is also very effective for Stop behaviours.

"In twenty seconds I am going to ask you to stop playing with my glasses." (Of course, if you are really worried that damage will be done, take immediate action!)

- To take the sting out of always having to follow adults' instructions, we need to inject an element of choice whenever possible. To simplify your life, limit the choices to two:

"I know you want to keep playing with that, but you can't. Would you like to hand it to me, or would you like to put it back on the shelf yourself?"

"Would you like to put the Lego™ away while I put the cars away, or would you like to tidy the cars while I put the Lego™ away?"

- Friendliness on our part often calls forth friendliness from the child. Knowing this, we can spend a minute or two being friendly, showing an interest in the positive part of what they are doing.

"Oh, those ornaments are so pretty and shiny. And you're being so careful. Now it's time to put them back."

"You've made a big city. It's got houses and roads and little people. This looks like a mum and dad and lots of kids. In two minutes I'm going to ask you to move your whole city back into your room because it's blocking the landing."

- Another way to help children want to co-operate is to show them that we understand how frustrated and annoyed they must feel when we interrupt their fun and tell them they need to do something different. This is called Reflective Listening:

"You've got so much energy and you love jumping. I know you wish you could jump on the sofa. But the rule is 'No playing on the furniture'."

"You're right in the middle of your game and you don't want to stop. It's hard to stop when you're having so much fun. And it took so long to set up your fort exactly right. You wish you didn't have to dismantle it before bedtime."

- We have seen how useless it is to expect co-operation from a child who is upset. First we must help him to *feel* more co-operative. Similarly, it is pointless to expect children to be their best selves when they are tired, hungry, hyperactive due to too much junk food or distracted by their Playstation™ beeping at them. If we want to make family life calmer, easier and happier we need to
  - put children to bed earlier
  - drastically limit the convenience food and comfort food they crave: high-sugar, high-salt and high-fat
  - drastically reduce the amount of time they spend in front of screens.

7 Transforming resistance

When your child is not complying with your instruction or not responding positively to your "seed planting" of what he should do, he will either be resisting noisily (screaming, crying, whingeing, arguing, pleading etc.) or he will be resisting more quietly (ignoring you, or trying to engage you in conversation about something else). The non-compliance seems, on the face of it, to be the child's fault. However, we need to remember that the child is responding in this manner for a reason. In the past this behaviour usually got him what he wanted: either your undivided attention, or a bit more time to do the forbidden activity or to not do what you want him to. It may even give him a feeling of power when he sees that he can wind up a parent.

Here is what does *not* work to influence your child towards co-operation:

- Giving in "for a quiet life". You won't get a quiet life! You will get less and less respect.
- Repeating, re-explaining, cajoling, bribing or threatening. These responses will undermine your authority and make you more and more "ignorable".
- Asking him why he is upset or why he doesn't want to do what you are telling him to do. He may know why or he may not. Even if he does know, he may not be able to articulate it clearly. And even if he can tell you, the discussion will weaken your message. Questioning your child

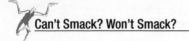

may give him the mistaken impression that if he can convince you that he has a good enough reason not to comply, he won't have to.

- Assuming he will continue to refuse. When a child says, "No, I won't" or throws himself on the floor in fury, it is much less serious than it sounds or looks. Usually, it just means that he doesn't feel like doing it at the moment. By using your new parenting skills, you will be able to harness the motivation to please that exists in all human beings.

- Allowing yourself to be drawn into an argument about why he should do it. A plaintive "Why do I have to?" is rarely a genuine request for information. If your instruction is a sensible one, the child usually understands why he should do it he, or he can easily work out why.

- Trying to get him to stop crying, whingeing, sulking or swearing. When we try, we are allowing ourselves to get distracted from the important issue, which is achieving co-operation. Children resort to these negative responses for a number of reasons:
    - The child may not know how else to express his anger, frustration or anxiety. If that is the case, it is our job to teach him to use words. Reflectively Listening, which I discuss later, is a useful skill for this.
    - The child may know *how* to control himself, but he has never formed the *habit* of controlling himself, probably because the negative parental responses got him attention or got him "his own way" for a bit longer. If this is the problem, it is the parent's job to ease the child into calmer, more considerate and more mature responses.

Following him if he storms out of the room. If you follow him, he's in charge. Let him go; he'll be back, usually within minutes. When he returns, he may try to act as if nothing happened, in the hopes that you will have forgotten. But you must not forget.

Here are some of the approaches that *do* work to help children move from unwilling to willing.

- Let him cry, whinge, or sulk, rather than trying to jolly him out of it or distract him or reason with him. Offer a hug, and Descriptively Praise any glimmers of positivity. Don't respond to the negative. It is perfectly natural and normal that children will not want to do everything that is asked of them. If we give the impression that their upset feelings are upsetting or worrying to us, we hand children the power to upset us.

This is a weapon that they can use against us whenever they are angry, out-of-sorts or just looking for a fun challenge.

- The occasional child calms down more quickly when left alone, but most children respond very well to a parental presence, as long as the parent is not lecturing, shouting or threatening. Sit near him, *saying very little*. When a child is upset, almost anything a parent says (other than giving in) will further inflame the situation. Instead, offer a hug.

- Reflectively listen to show your child that you care about his feelings:
  - "I can see you're really angry. You don't want to tidy up. You wish you could keep playing."
  - "Maybe it feels embarrassing to say goodbye to our guest. You wish you didn't have to."

  Don't worry that statements like these will mislead your children into thinking he does not need to comply. The word "wish" clearly conveys that it is a fantasy, not a real option.

- It should go without saying that if a child attempts to hurt someone (even himself) or to damage property (even his own) he should be stopped immediately. Of course we will use the minimum force necessary, but we must not be afraid to take immediate, decisive action to restrain the child. When children are allowed to be destructive, it only makes them feel worse. They often feel deep shame, an emotion that is so uncomfortable that they try to cancel it out by justifying their actions. They also are angry at the adults whose weakness led to them feeling so bad. If you have a child who is physically or verbally aggressive, take heart. The more you put all these strategies into place, the more your child will show you his best side.

When the child finally complies we need to reinforce his eventual co-operation:

- Show how pleased you are.
- He may still be upset, even though he did what you asked of him. As soon as he is in a calmer mood, do one or more Action Replays. Do this before talking about anything else, before letting him do anything, before doing anything for him. In the Action Replay you and the child replay the scenario, but this time the child does the right thing straightaway, with no fuss. Let's say, for example, that you said "It's bedtime" (after having eased him into the transition with a count-down, of course) and at first your child argued or ignored you, but

eventually he complied. As soon as he is over his upset, you can say to him: "Now we'll do an Action Replay (or a do-over, or whatever you want to call it). I'll tell you it's bedtime and this time you won't argue. What will you do instead?" The child will probably respond with "I'll just go upstairs" or "I'll say O.K.". As a result of this little talk-through (during which you ask the questions and the child answers) you will be sure he knows the appropriate responses and actions. At that point, you both act it out. You say "It's bedtime" and your child says something like "All right" and then he goes up the stairs. An Action Reply can be done at any time, even the following day. Action Replays are very powerful because they wipe the slate clean so that the incident ends on a positive note. Having your child practise the right way to respond will influence his future behaviour far more effectively than parental lectures can.

On very, very rare occasions a child who has eventually complied will show us that he is still angry, either by refusing outright to do the Action Replay or by being silly and not doing it properly. Don't try to insist. Remember my earlier advice about not giving a direct instruction until we are almost certain that the child will co-operate. Instead, you can say, "I can see you're not quite ready to do the Action Replay. I'll ask you again in a few minutes". And in the meantime nothing fun happens, not even an interesting conversation, not even a snack. Hugs, however, are always appropriate when a child is upset.

Start and stop behaviours

You may want your child to stop a certain misbehaviour and also to start doing something completely unrelated. For example, you may want him to stop whingeing for another biscuit and to start putting his toys away.

If your child is in a co-operative mood, you can tackle the Start behaviour first. When he complies, this will distract him from the Stop behaviour. However, if your child is not in a positive frame of mind, for your sanity tackle the Stop behaviour first. That behaviour will need to stop before the child will be even remotely interested in paying attention to what you have to say about the Start behaviour.

Chapter 13
Crisis management for Stop behaviours

When we are busy or stressed, we may be tempted to just bellow "Stop that" or to simply call out the child's name or to say "No!" or "Don't do that!" We assume that the child knows what he should stop doing. He may know, but our sharp or annoyed tone will not help him want to co-operate. And it is quite possible that he does *not* know exactly what he is doing wrong.

- When we need to curtail our children's fun, we can show our goodwill by helping them think about alternative activities. Rather than expecting them to suppress their childish urges, we can help re-channel them more appropriately:

    "Your new drum sounds just like a real drum in a band. You know how to make a very big noise. But the rule is 'Quiet indoors'. I know you love drumming. Let's think about where you could do your drumming that's not inside the flat".

    "I can see you're really interested in that sharp knife, and you want to hold it. But you know the rule. 'We don't play with knives'. But tonight you can use the knife to help me cut the quiche. I know you can be very careful with the sharp knife. And I'll be there to help you and make sure everyone stays safe."

- It helps to depersonalise our instruction when we state it as a family rule that applies equally to all:
    - "We have to use inside voices when we are inside the flat. Mummy has to, and so does Daddy, and so do you. We all have to talk quietly."
    - "The Jones family has a very important rule: No hurting or frightening the cats."

- Rather than attributing malicious intent, we can view our children's misbehaviour as a childish mistake:
    - "You didn't mean to push her over. You were just running past. That's why we have a rule: 'No running in the house'."

- It is more effective to say what the child should be doing than to say what he should not. It becomes even more effective when we also demonstrate the right action. As soon as the child copies us we can Descriptively Praise him:

- "Stroke the kitten gently. Very softly, like this… You're being so gentle now. That's what the kitten likes."

- Of course, our aim with all the above strategies is for the child to stop the misbehaviour straight away. For some children that is just not possible, even when they are very motivated to comply. In general, children tend to have a slower reaction time than adults have. And this is especially true of children who fall into the difficult or slow-to-warm up temperament categories.

  - Such a child's movements and reaction time can be very speedy, indeed hyperactive, when he is engaged in (or going towards) something that appeals to him, but slow, distracted and even lethargic when faced with an activity that he does not want to do. This can be very puzzling to parents. It seems as if the delay must be deliberate. Sometimes, of course, it may be deliberate. But more often than not the slow reaction time is constitutional. So our goal, when addressing Stop behaviours, is for the child to stop as quickly as he personally is able to.

  - Depending on his innate reaction time, the child who intends to comply with an instruction or to a "seed planting" will start moving in the right direction within one to ten seconds. If he does not "start to stop" within that time, then parents need to take immediate action, while stating the rule calmly but strongly. Of course we feel completely comfortable about taking immediate action when a child's safety is in danger. But following through straightaway is just as important when the issue is not safety but co-operation.

    If the child does not start to stop quite quickly, taking nto account his natural reaction time, resist the impulse to simply repeat louder, or re-explain, threaten or cajole. Your child will probably ignore your second statement, and the third and the fourth, just as he did the first, unless you add action to your words. The action that you take can either be removing an object from the child or removing the child from the situation. As soon as you make a move to follow through in this way, probably your child will see that you mean business and will instantly comply. At this point parents generally abort the follow-through. Their reasoning is that the child complied so no further parental input is necessary. But now is the perfect time to reinforce co-operation with Descriptive Praise and Reflective Listening:

"I'm so glad I didn't have to put that game up on the shelf for the rest of the day. You stopped playing with the game so quickly, even though you were having fun. And I only had to say it once."

"You really wanted another biscuit, but you only had two because that's what I said, only two. You did just what I told you."

Parents hope that talking about the possible consequences of non-co-operation will motivate children. In fact, threats frequently make the child more rebellious. Here is a different approach that is more effective:

- Think, and talk, about rewards rather than about consequences or punishments.
- Only mention the possible reward *before* you give the instruction, while you are planting the seed or doing a talk-through. Once you have stated clearly exactly what you want your child to do, any continued talk of rewards will seem like pleading and will undermine your authority. A reward is only a "sweetener"; it provides a *bit* of extra motivation. We must not abdicate our authority by expecting the potential reward to convince the child to co-operate. As I have shown, we need to put lots of time and thought into presenting a United Front, clarifying our rules, keeping calm and smiling, arranging the environment so that it becomes easier for the child to behave well than to misbehave, etc., etc.
- When a chronically non-compliant child co-operates eventually (but not immediately) he deserves a small reward that reinforces for him that we are pleased. These small tokens of our appreciation can be ladled out scores of times a day:
  - Descriptive Praise
  - a smile
  - a hug
  - the thumbs-up sign or some other gesture of approval.
- A slightly more substantial reward is in order when the same child co-operates immediately. We want to make a big deal about this relatively rare occurrence:
  - staying up an extra 5 to 10 minutes after the usual bedtime
  - an extra story or song at bedtime
  - a choice about something that is usually chosen for him.

When parents are interacting with a sensitive, intense, impulsive child, they find themselves replying "No, you can't" to many requests, pleas and complaints.

"Can I have another biscuit?"

"Will you play with me?"

"Can you give me a lift to the shops?"

"I never get to sit there."

"The wings keep falling off."

"I want chips, not mash."

"Tie my shoes."

"I can't do this sum."

When we answer "No", the child, impatient, disappointed, frustrated or angry, does not want to give up easily. He may fall back on a wide repertoire of reactions that have been effective in the past at getting his parents to change their minds, at least some of the time. He may whinge, nag, sulk, cry, shout, insult or even kick. These reactions are, of course, Stop behaviours, and must be dealt with and stopped before there can be any discussion about what the child has asked for. If we allow ourselves to be drawn into talking about the content of the request while the child is still misbehaving, we are unintentionally sending the message that it is acceptable for him to react in that way. See Chapter 12 for strategies that will help a child who is in this state to calm down and become more co-operative.

In addition, we have it in our power to reduce the intensity of the child's negative reaction:

- Stop and think before you say "No". If you suspect that you might be tempted to change your mind after a while, do not say "No" in the first place. You may convince yourself that you are changing your mind because you have carefully re-considered the evidence or because you want to show that you are being flexible or fair. But from the child's point of view, he nagged you and you gave in. You can't blame him for storing this experience away in his long-term memory and trying it on again… and again.
- Smile and stay friendly.
- Feel free to say "I haven't decided yet. I'll let you know in a few minutes". It is very useful for impulsive, intense children to learn to be patient. To make sure that the child doesn't keep asking or pestering you, a good rule is "If you talk about it anymore before I say yes or no, my answer will definitely be *no*". If you are willing to stick to this, you will find that very soon your child will start thinking before he speaks.
- Instead of focusing on the "No", you can convey the same information using a "Yes" attitude and modelling how he can use problem-solving to get at least some of what he wants:

- Instead of saying

    "No more biscuits. You'll ruin your appetite."

  you could say,

    "Yes, you can have another biscuit after dinner."

- Instead of

    "I don't have time to play."

  this sounds friendlier:

    "I'd love to play with you for ten minutes. I'll be ready as soon as the laundry is folded. Would you like to help so it goes faster?"

- Instead of

    "You're old enough to tie your own shoes."

  this response would be more helpful:

    "I know you can do some of it. I'll watch while you tie the first knot. Then you watch while I tie the bow. And I'll show you how I get it really tight so it stays tied."

- Instead of

    "No, how many times have I told you!"

  this response is gentler:

    "My job is to take care of your health. That's why we have a rule: sweets only once a week. Three more days to go."

- Before the child even has a chance to work himself up into a tantrum, use the skill called Reflective Listening to show him that you can see how hard it is for him to accept this disappointment. Our compassion costs us nothing, and it takes some of the sting out of it for the child:

    "You're so keen to show me the city you built, and now you're going to have to wait because I'm not ready. That's really disappointing for you. And maybe you're worried I'll forget all about it."

    "I can see how angry you're feeling. That wing keeps falling off – so frustrating. You're wishing I could fix it, even though I said I won't because it will just fall off again."

- Even if the child is reacting in an unacceptable way, we can look for and Descriptively Praise small bits of O.K. behaviour, or even the momentary absence of the negative behaviour.

    "That's a friendlier voice. So now I can listen."

    "You're not trying to grab it away from me. Thanks."

    "I don't hear any swearing. You're being respectful now."

Descriptive Praise is not a magic wand that will instantly eradicate all the children's uncomfortable feelings. A chronically angry child might even respond to Descriptively Praise by immediately resuming the crying or complaining, just to prove you wrong.

A parent might conclude from the child's negative response that Descriptive Praise is a bad idea. But don't give up! Descriptive Praise will influence him, gradually, to become calmer, friendlier, more willing, even more mature.

Parents sometimes struggle for years to get their children into the habit of asking *politely* for what they want. The main problems are whingeing and not saying "please" or "thank you". What does *not* work, in the long term, is to prompt him when he forgets by saying, for example, "Say that nicely, please" or "What's the magic word?" These prompts do not help the child's long-term memory to get the message that polite requests are important. In fact, quite the opposite is true. The prompts merely serve to rescue the child from the real-life consequences of not communicating respectfully. A more useful response is:

> "You didn't say 'please' so the answer is no. You can ask me again after dinner (or in five minutes, or tomorrow, etc.), and I'm sure you'll remember to say 'please'."

> "That wasn't your friendly voice (or polite or respectful, or whatever term you use in your family) so the answer is no. In a few minutes you can try again. Probably you won't whinge next time."

> And if your child does not yet know how long it takes for a certain number of minutes to elapse, get a timer. Remember, no discussion. And of course, the rule about "Repeating automatically turns a maybe into a no" still stands.

As for "thank you", two strategies are effective. One is to hang on to whatever you are handing your child until he says "thank you", and then of course Descriptively Praise him for remembering to. The other strategy is to reply to a request with "No, because the last time I said yes (or the last time I gave you a biscuit, etc.) you didn't say "thank you". This response will definitely motivate him to take you seriously.

Chapter 14
Crisis management for Start behaviours

The purpose of discipline is to help our children develop the habits of co-operation, confidence, motivation, self-reliance and consideration.

The Six-Step Method, which should be used for Start behaviours only, helps children achieve these habits more effectively than any other strategy I know. Use this method when the child is not doing anything wrong, but you want him to start doing something else. The method combines a number of the Calmer, Easier, Happier Parenting skills:

- Being in charge
- Preparing for success
- Positive communication
- Providing a sensible lifestyle
- Paying attention to details
- Making the time and taking the time
- Descriptive Praise
- Reflective Listening
- Following through.

Over the years, you may have grown accustomed to your child ignoring your instructions or arguing back. Even though you want the situation to change, you may find it very hard to believe that these six simple steps, or indeed any strategy, can, over a short while, achieve calm co-operation.

This method achieves its aims so well because it gives children what they need. It is positive (calm, friendly, respectful), and firm (clear, definite, determined, with follow-through). Consistency comes when you use the Six-Step Method for all Start behaviours.

Until parents try this method they may believe that they do not have the time in their busy days to spend on all these steps. But very soon they see for themselves how much hassle, and therefore how much time, is saved when children get used to co-operating the first time they are asked, and without a fuss.

For a relatively easy-going child, the Six-Step Method is much less necessary, although it is still useful. Even as a toddler, the easy-going child soon drifts into the habit of co-operation. It is the sensitive, intense, impulsive child who particularly needs to be helped to develop the habit of co-operation.

Sometimes parents object initially to the Six-Step Method because it seems an unnecessary "palaver"; they feel that the child should respect the parent and just obey, without needing a special method to make it happen.

Even though it would be nice if children automatically respected their parents, we know that there is a sizeable minority of children who do not. As adults, we only respect someone who has earned our respect. The same is true for children and teenagers. They will respect us when we have earned their respect. The positive, firm and consistent strategies in this book will help your child to listen to you, take you seriously and do what you say – in other words, to respect you.

Here is a thorough explanation of each of the steps in the Six-Step-Method. You will notice that with this method, the parent does not even give the instruction until Step 3.

Step 1: Stop what you are doing, stand near your child and look at him

If we ourselves do not take our instruction seriously enough to stop what we are doing and go to the child and look at him, we cannot be surprised if he does not really take it seriously either.

If we want our children to listen and take in what we say, we must not call up the stairs or from one room to the next, or even from one side of the room to the other.

When we stand very near to a child, he cannot block us out for long, even if he is trying hard to ignore us. Occasionally a parent is concerned that standing very close will be experienced by the child as intimidating or as an invasion of "personal space". That might be true if you were being annoyed or critical. But the six steps are all very positive, as you will see. Standing (when one could sit) demonstrates intentionality, determination, a sense of "This is important", whereas sitting conveys a more relaxed attitude. Our eye contact also demonstrates to the child that "This is important".

Step 2: Wait until your child stops what he is doing and looks at you

This is how you capture your child's attention. It is the opposite of what so often happens. If you were to give your instruction while the child was still focused on whatever he was doing, he might not hear you. Even if he did hear you, he might forget very quickly because he would not be taking you seriously. The child's attitude changes dramatically when we are willing to stand and wait until he looks up.

At first the child may pretend that he does not realise you are there. He may assume, from past experience, that you have come to tell him off, so he may be attempting to put off the dreaded moment. But when he hears no telling off, he relaxes, and his natural urge to communicate with a loved one rises to the surface. The more often you use the Six-Step Method for Start behaviours, the more your child will naturally want to look at you and listen to you.

Do *not* call the child's name to get his attention. Mostly, a child hears his name when we are telling him to do something or not to do something. He tries to tune this out, so calling his name rarely gets his real attention or his motivation.

Do not attempt to employ the Six-Step Method when your child is watching television or on the computer. Screen activity can be so mesmerising and so addictive, especially for a child with a sensitive, intense, impulsive temperament, that he may not be tempted ever to look at you, no matter how long you wait.

You will need to get all electronics switched off before you even start Step 1. Let us assume that your child has been given permission to be on the computer or Game Boy™ or television for a certain length of time, and now the time is up.

1 Give him a count-down about five minutes before.

2 Keep track of the time!

3 Go to him and say *once* "Now it is time to switch off," or similar words, and require him to respond to you in words (not a grunt) as well as by action.

4 Taking into account his natural reaction speed, give him a few seconds to comply. If he does, be very pleased. If he does not switch off, take immediate action and switch it off yourself.

While you are waiting for your child to stop what he is doing and look at you, show an interest in whatever he is doing and find something to Descriptively Praise. This will motivate him to return your eye contact and will help him to feel friendlier and more willing to listen. For example:

"That puzzle has a lot of pieces. And you haven't given up."
"Those blocks are balanced so carefully. That's a tall tower."

Step 3: Give the instruction – clearly, simply and only once

Only at Step 3 is the parent finally able to give the instruction. During the time it takes to accomplish Steps 1 and 2 the parent has time to consider carefully: Is this instruction worth saying? Do I have the time and energy to follow through? The parent also has time to focus on becoming calm, friendly and polite and on how to phrase the instruction positively. We want our children to learn to be polite, so we need, at the very least, to lead by example.

Having given the instruction clearly and simply, do *not* repeat yourself. If you do, you are sending the message that the children need not listen the first time, or possibly even the fourth.

You may worry that you would be forced to repeat your instruction because the child might not have heard you the first time. But in Step 2 you waited for him to look at you, so you definitely know that he is listening. It might happen that as you are telling him what to do his attention wanders and he looks away. Stop talking instantly and remain standing and waiting. When he looks back at you (which he will do to see why you stopped speaking) Descriptively Praise him for looking at you. Then start talking again. As long as you stay positive and respectful, your child will find it easy to listen. Children are genetically programmed to take their parents seriously, unless we put a spanner in the works with our inconsistency, nagging, shouting … or smacking.

If you are the parent of a child who often disobeys or simply ignores your instructions, you will find it hard to believe that these first three steps will results in co-operation 95% of the time. Most of the time you will not even need Steps 4, 5 and 6. At this point you may be thinking, "But my child is different. He's much more rebellious, (or sensitive, or argumentative or mischievous or manipulative). This method won't work with him".

You are basing that assumption on how your child has been reacting to your old methods. But the Six-Step Method is radically different. It works by influencing over time, rather than trying to control through anger. It is friendly and respectful. It does not hurry the child. It gives parents the time to calm down and think about how to be most effective.

This method works to build the habit of co-operation and much sooner than parents might think possible. Most children will comply after Step 3, but luckily we still have three more steps, to mop up any remaining opposition.

Step 4

Ask the child to repeat the instruction back to you – accurately, thoroughly and in his own words.

When the child does this, you have indisputable proof that he has heard you and that he understands exactly what he must do. And he knows that you know that he knows. This eliminates a lot of the excuses.

Do not allow him to parrot back the words he just heard you say. Many children can do this without really registering what they need to do. The child's brain responds very differently when he has to put the instruction into words of his own choosing. He will automatically be forming a mental picture of himself doing the next activity.

There is another advantage to having your child tell you in his own words what he has to do. When he hears himself saying it, he takes it far more seriously. In a subtle way he feels morally obligated to do what he himself has said he would do, whereas he is used to disregarding what the adults say.

Essentially Step 4 is a mini-talk-through. It trains the child in self-reliance.

If you arrange your child's life so that it is governed by predictable routines, a very interesting thing will start happening more and more. After doing Steps 1 and 2, even before you give your instruction in Step 3, the child will pre-empt you. He may say "I know, I know, it's bedtime" or "Is it teatime?" You will often find that you can skip straight from Step 2 to Step 4. This is further training for the child in using his own brain, rather than relying on an adult to tell him what to do.

Step 5: Stand and wait

This may feel tough because in a busy household there is always something you need to be doing, some mini-crisis to sort out. But if you have a child who is not yet in the habit of co-operating 95% of the time, *this* is the mini-crisis that needs your attention more than any other. Think of the time you spend standing and waiting as an investment that will very soon pay off in a calmer, easier, happier family life.

You may be imagining that you will have to stand and wait for hours! You are remembering all those times when your child kept disregarding what you said so in frustration you resorted to repeating, nagging, complaining and finally shouting. It may be hard to accept that it is those very parental reactions, what I call verbal smacking, that cause a lot of the non-co-operation. When we are polite, respectful, calm, clear and determined, children naturally want to please us.

Of course, this method works more quickly with some children than with others. The child who has been angry for a long time will take longer to learn to trust and respect us. The sensitive, intense, impulsive child is often more stubborn and more explosive. What about the child who is used to unclear rules and routines and inconsistent follow-through? He will test again and again before he really sees that this new method is here to stay. When you commit to standing and waiting, it is not long before your child senses that you mean business.

To make the necessary standing and waiting less stressful for you, make a point of starting all your routine activities earlier so that you have time to spare, rather than feeling that you are always hurrying to beat the clock. Giving yourself more time is particularly helpful in relieving the stress of getting everyone out of the house on school mornings. When parents are contemplating the idea of getting up earlier in the mornings, it initially fills them with dread: "I'm tired all the time as it is! I can't afford to shave another twenty minutes off my sleeping time." However, as soon as parents start getting up earlier, they universally report feeling *more* rested because they are so much less stressed when the morning mayhem is significantly reduced.

Step 6: While you are standing and waiting: Descriptively Praise every step in the right direction, no matter how small. Also Reflectively Listen to how the child might be feeling about what you have asked him to do

The purpose of the Descriptive Praise is to show the child that we like him and approve of him. You might not think this is necessary. But especially when we have a history of nagging and shouting, the child may come to expect a heated, upsetting interaction, rather than a calm, friendly one.

Descriptive Praise, as I have shown earlier, is the most powerful motivator and training tool. Examples of Descriptively Praising a tiny step in the right direction might he:

> "Thanks for not arguing."
> "You've put your Barbie down."
> "You're closer to the door."

We could even Descriptively Praise *past* good behaviour:

> "You're getting quicker and quicker at doing what you're told."
> "I hardly heard you shouting today."

Reflective Listening is the skill we use to show that we care about our children's feelings, not just about whether they do what they are told. Reflective Listening shows that we understand that he may not want to stop what he is doing and move on to the next activity. For example, we might say:

> "You're having so much fun building with your new set. You don't want to stop."

> "It's not easy to tidy up when you want to keep playing."

And we can combine Descriptive Praise and Reflective Listening for maximum impact:

> "Even though you probably wish I would just leave you alone, you're not arguing and you haven't told me to get out."

> "I know you're really annoyed that it's bedtime already, but you're not shouting or being rude."

What if the child storms off during any of the steps? Do not follow him. Just go about your life; do not feel that you have to stay rooted to the spot. Start again from Step 1 when he next comes to you, which will happen sooner that you might think.

What if he cries, complains, insults, sulks, etc.? Persevere with the 6 steps. I can guarantee you that the Six-Step Method *always* works. That is because there is no Step 7 which says: "After a while, give up". If you persevere calmly, respectfully, quietly and firmly, your child's natural inbuilt desire to please you will nudge him, more and more often, to do the right thing.

Chapter 15
Conclusion

Here are the experiences of some parents who have chosen to make these new skills a way of life:

> *"I used to feel very tense, never knowing what kind of a mood my son would be in. He could be charming or he could be grumpy and defiant. It is no exaggeration to say that Descriptive Praise and talk-throughs have changed our lives. He's so much calmer and more confident. And so am I."*

> *"It's been a hard year for us: major illness in the family, being made redundant, having to re-train. At first my wife and I found we were taking it out on the children, snapping at them and getting very irritated. Through the "Calmer, Easier, Happier Parenting" methods we have earned how to be less stressed and more positive. We made a promise to ourselves to Descriptively Praise each family member ten times a day for a month. The results were even better than we could have hoped for. The children are happier and more co-operative. They're even doing better at school. Descriptive Praise is a way of life for us now."*

> *"At first I was very sceptical about Descriptive Praise and all the other strategies because I thought I'd never be able to keep it up. But the children responded so quickly that I was very motivated to do it more and more. My son is less anxious and more self-reliant; my daughter isn't so bossy any more, so now the other girls want to play with her. And the children do what they're told, first time! Bliss! I still have to pinch myself sometimes."*

Would you like to experience a similar transformation? The only difference between these families and yours is that these parents started practising some new skills and didn't give up. With the same determination, you and your children can experience a calmer, easier, happier family life.

Appendix
The legal debate

Arguments for and against passing a law that would ban all physical punishment

Of course, those who defend the occasional, mild smack will not be in favour of a law that bans all forms of corporal punishment. Interestingly, even amongst those who are completely against smacking, opinion is strongly divided as to whether a legal ban would be useful.

Arguments against the proposed law

1 Those who are against a total ban on smacking point out that we do already have on our books laws that outlaw violence towards children and therefore we do not need the proposed new law.

2 There is a worry that technically such a law would criminalise parents for the occasional slap. This could, theoretically, clog up the courts and waste a lot of taxpayers' money. It would also undermine parents' confidence in their ability to make decisions about how to bring up their children.

3 Some people are concerned that a legal ban would further erode the increasingly unstable balance of power between parent and child. We already hear of children who jokingly threaten to ring and report their parents to Childline when a privilege is withdrawn or they are shouted at. Even though a child may say this in jest, the joke can make parents uneasy because it would be so easy for the child to do, and the consequences could be dire.

4 By itself, the law would neither promote nor teach more effective strategies for influencing children's behaviour.

5 Nor would it teach parents how to reduce the stresses that are the inevitable precursors to extreme punishment.

6 At present, public opinion is still weighted towards smacking, and it is notoriously difficult to enforce an unpopular law.

7 It is not possible to legislate changes in popular opinion.

8 The new law would focus all the attention and all the responsibility for curbing smacking on the parents. This is a simplistic attitude as physical punishment is most prevalent amongst families who are barely

coping under severe, sustained stress. Several of the following stress factors are usually present, often entrenched, stretching back several generations:

- Disturbed employment profiles, which might be unemployment, under-employment, or erratic employment, but also over-employment, which keeps parents away from home for long hours, often resulting in children becoming adept at negative attention-seeking
- Crowded, sub-standard housing
- Chronic illness or disability, including mental health vulnerability
- Domestic violence
- Ignorance of the normal needs of children at each developmental stage
- Ignorance of alternative methods of discipline
- Ignorance of a healthy lifestyle
- Substance misuse
- Functional illiteracy
- Poverty
- Single-parent families or blended families
- Children with subtle specific learning difficulties who are experiencing school problems, whether academically, behaviourally or socially.

Any welfare-state government that assumes it has the right to legislate on family matters should also be expected to shoulder the responsibility for effectively addressing these issues in order to support families and safeguard the wellbeing of society's most vulnerable members, our children.

Arguments for the proposed law

1 The law that has until recently been on the books dates from 1860, and states:

> "A parent....may for the purpose of correcting what is evil in the child, inflict moderate and reasonable corporal punishment."

Do we really still believe that misbehaviour is due to evil that lurks somewhere inside a child? According to the opinion polls, overwhelmingly we do not believe this. Following recent legal battles, the government and the majority of people polled readily acknowledge that this archaic concept does not provide adequate protection and therefore accept that reform is overdue. For example, most people nowadays are keen to ban smacking with objects, smacking on the head or face, smacking that leaves a mark or causes mental harm and the smacking of infants below a certain age. Let us take this opportunity not just to tinker with the law and amend it slightly, but to make an absolutely clear statement.

2 It is unlawful to assault an adult. Surely our children, infinitely more fragile and more vulnerable, deserve equal protection under the law.

3 To date, eight European countries have taken the brave step of banning all physical punishment of children (Austria, Croatia, Cyprus, Denmark, Finland, Latvia, Norway and Sweden). Some statisticians claim (and others hotly deny the claim) that the total ban in those countries has resulted in a dramatic reduction in assaults against children, fewer child fatalities due to violence, fewer formal interventions and fewer children being taken into care. The statistics appear to be inconclusive, and can, like most statistics, be interpreted in several different ways, depending on what point one is trying to make. What is indisputable is that public attitudes towards smacking shifted rapidly once those countries adopted the bans.

4 Some say that wholesale reform is not needed because smacking as a regular practice is dying out anyway. Unfortunately, recent government-sponsored research does not substantiate this optimistic view. Three-quarters of the mothers sampled in the research had smacked their babies before the age of one year old. A third of the parents interviewed said they smacked their children weekly or even more often, sometimes severely and sometimes with an object.

5 Those who favour a total ban say that legal acceptance of any degree of corporal punishment creates a grey area where abuse can creep in and take hold. The law, as it currently exists, aims to protect children from harm; inconsistent legal judgements have created dangerous confusion about where to draw the line. It is reported that a few schools have got round the institutional ban by inviting parents into school to smack their child for a school transgression.

6 Even if not completely enforceable, a total ban would send a much stronger message than at present that violence against children is unacceptable. Making an action illegal does not, of course, instantly or automatically change cultural norms. But it has been proven that legal reforms do, over time, significantly influence the public's perception of what is acceptable and unacceptable.

7 Proponents of the proposed law are quick to offer reassurance that the courts would not be interested in pursuing legal action against well-

meaning parents who give the occasional smack. That would not be in anyone's interests. The purpose of the law would be educational, not punitive. This law would be administered in a similar manner as the law that outlaws physical violence between adults. Every fight does not come into court, just the most extreme instances of physical aggression.

8 Physical restraint is not the same as physical punishment. Even with a total ban on smacking, parents will of course be able to physically restrain their children, for example to keep them out of danger.

9 Once this law is passed, government agencies at every level will be forced to focus, much more than at present, on promoting more effective ways of discipline:
   - disseminating information more widely, through more channels
   - teaching parents, caregivers and teachers
   - supporting parents who find it difficult, for whatever reason, to adopt new methods.

10 With regard to the concern that angry children might misuse the law to get their well-intentioned parents arrested, I personally am not worried. In my observation, when children are prompted to take, or even to seriously consider, such an extreme measure, it is always because there has been a painful, often traumatic breakdown in family communication. The involvement of an outside agency can be helpful, if only as a wake-up call, even though the stigma may be difficult to come to terms with.

11 The alternative to a complete ban would be to attempt to legislate exactly who is allowed to smack whom, when and how, on which parts of the body, how often and how hard. That would be a minefield; no one would be able to agree. For example, would adults other than the biological parents be allowed to smack the child? Would a step-parent of many years be entitled? A new step-parent? An unmarried partner? A live-in boyfriend? At what age could a child be smacked? But what if that child is disabled? Already the issue of bruising has caused argument. The law has now outlawed any smacks that are hard enough to leave a visible bruise. But some have countered that because dark skin masks bruising, parents of dark-skinned children will be legally allowed to smack them harder.

And so the debate continues. It is having the effect of raising public awareness, encouraging people to examine and clarify their values and focusing attention and government resources on promoting gentler and more effective methods of discipline.